## It's Time to Take
## THE NATIONS!

# SHEEP
# NATIONS

**AUTHOR OF *THE HEALING POWER OF THE ROOTS***

# DOMINIQUAE
# BIERMAN, PHD

SHEEP NATIONS © 2003-2020 by Dominique Bierman. All rights reserved.

This book may not be copied or reprinted for commercial gain or profit. The use of short quotations or occasional page copying for personal or group study is permitted and encouraged. Permission will be granted upon request.

Unless otherwise identified, all Scripture quotations are from the *New King James Version*. Copyright © 1982 by *Thomas Nelson, Inc*. Used by permission. All rights reserved.

Words such as Jesus, Christ, LORD and God have been changed by the author back to their original Hebrew renderings: Yeshua, Yahveh and ELOHIM.

Paperback ISBN: 978-1-953502-25-4
E-Book ISBN: 978-1-953502-26-1

First Printing July 2003, Second Printing August 2005, Third Printing December 2020

Published by *Zion's Gospel Press* | shalom@zionsgospel.com

Kad-Esh MAP Ministries
52 Tuscan Way, Ste 202-412, St. Augustine, Florida 32092, USA
www.kad-esh.org

ZIONS GOSPEL
PRESS

*To the ashes of my people in Auschwitz. For the sin of silence, for the sin of indifference; for the sin of secret complicity of the neutral; for the closing of borders; for the washing of hands; for all that was done; for all not done.*

*Like an earring of gold and an ornament of fine gold is a wise rebuker to an obedient ear.*

PROVERBS 25:12

## Early Messianic Symbol

This sign has been found in pottery and on walls of what is believed to be the meeting rooms of second-century believers in Jerusalem. During an archeological excavation in recent years, repeatedly found is this symbol (with variations).

Experts feel this symbol was a sign of unity between the Jewish believers and their Christian brethren in the rest of the Roman Empire. Some suggest that it was also a secret symbol of identification in times of persecution.

CONTENTS

**Introduction:** It's Time to Take the Nations! .................... 1

**Chapter 1:** A Visitation in Chile ............................. 7

**Chapter 2:** Give Me Sheep Nations!. ....................... 19

**Chapter 3:** The Church Must Repent First .................... 25

**Chapter 4:** The Heavenly Constitution ....................... 35

**Chapter 5:** The Key of Abraham ............................. 45

**Chapter 6:** Choosing the Blessing or the Curse for Your Nation . . 53

**Chapter 7:** Turn the Key of Abraham Into the Blessing Position. . 65

**Chapter 8:** The Blessing of Abraham – Full Wages! ............. 79

**Chapter 9:** The Master's Key For Greatness. .................... 95

**Chapter 10:** Dream Sheep Nations Into Existence. ........... 103

**Foreclosure:** End Word ....................................... 113

**Appendix I:** 2017 Anti-semitism Report. ..................... 115

**Appendix II:** Two Weddings and One Divorce ................. 137

INTRODUCTION

# It's Time to Take the Nations!

*The vision of ministering redemption to entire nations rather than only to individuals is an apostolic End time vision.*
— DOMINIQUAE BIERMAN

I always say that I know I am among apostolic people when I see the quantity of international flags and world maps on the walls of their sanctuary and offices. I also know that these apostolic people are on target, when I see the map of Israel and the flag of Israel in a prominent place. Israel is the *center piece* for the redemption of the nations. Once you are able to connect properly with Israel, Jerusalem, and the different covenants given to Israel, then you will be on your way to becoming part of the greatest *apostolic move that the world has ever seen*. I call it a MAP movement, which means "Messianic, apostolic, prophetic" movement. Of course, the MAP stands for the world map, as this present-day movement will gain momentum and will encompass the whole world. This move is not for the fearful, neither for those that resist change. It is also not for the prideful because it will require much humility to go through a *complete metamorphosis,* a transformation in your thinking and the way that you see faith in Messiah. This is also a *move of reformation and of restoration.* The Holy Spirit has been restoring the church, the *ecclesia,* into its original foundation with Israel, the Jewish people and the ancient Hebrew Scriptures, commonly and mistakenly called, the "Old Testament."

After the Council of Nicaea in AD 325, the church took a wrong turn that thrusted her into the Dark Ages and into *deep sin and deception.* Yahveh in His mercy has been taking her out of this pit, prepared by the enemy, back into truth-holiness-power, without which she cannot be the apostolic or MAP kind of church that she needs to be, in order to see the nations come into the kingdom and Israel saved.

For those that humble their hearts to this metamorphosis, cleansing and restoration, there will be a glorious empowering for the End time work that is at hand. And, they will be followed with amazing signs, wonders and miracles! I suggest that you read my book *The Healing Power of the Roots* in order to help you with the metamorphosis and reformation.

## VOCABULARY

Before you begin to read this book I would like you to be familiar with some renewed terminology that will help your understanding. In any new move of God, there is new or renewed terminology introduced. It is no different in the case of this End time move of restoration.

Here are four terms which are used throughout the entire book I would like you to be familiar with.

## Yahveh

*Yahveh* is the name of the Lord as revealed to Moses and used throughout the prophetic writings. *Yahveh* means the "I AM" and the "Ever-Present God."

This name is often used in conjunction with the name: Elohim, which is the name of the "Creator God."

## Yahveh Elohim

This is Hebrew for, *"The I AM who is the Creator."* The short way of saying Yahveh is Yah, as in Halelu-*Yah*. So, many times I will use the word Yah instead of "God."

## The Torah

*Torah* is the Hebrew word for "instruction in righteousness," commonly called "Law."

In this book Torah only refers to the Law of Yahveh in the Five Books of Moses and Law throughout the Bible. In this book, the Torah does not apply to rabbinical laws or manmade traditions. In a place where I mention a rabbinical tradition I will refer to it as such.

The Torah includes three types of charges:
- Commandments
- Statutes or Judgments
- Laws or Precepts

**Because that Abraham obeyed My voice, and kept My charge, My Commandments, My statutes, and My Laws.**

**Genesis 26:5**

Notice that before Moses was given the Torah at Mount Sinai, Abraham already walked and obeyed the Torah. Abraham already followed the Torah since the Torah of the Living Yah (God) is eternal.

The Commandments are eternal (referring to the Ten Commandments).

- The Statutes are also eternal and connected with holiness and worship. (Note: following the Statutes connected with Temple Worship requires more background knowledge. Since we are now the Temple of the Holy Spirit, an interpretation from the Holy Spirit is needed about how to follow them today.)
- The Precepts are eternal principles though the actual instructions were temporary and only relevant to the issues of the times they were given. So, today we keep the principles and apply them to our times. As we walk with the Holy Spirit of Yah He continues to give us precepts daily!

Here is the ticket to lifelong success and prosperity.

**This Book of the Law (Torah) shall not depart from your mouth, but you shall meditate in it day and night, that you may observe to do according to all that is written in it. For then you will make your way prosperous, and then you will have good success.**

**Joshua 1:8**

Abraham who is the father of the faith, understood and walked in the way which he had been given. Also in these End times the Torah is being restored: A revelation by the Holy Spirit to the church. As we meditate in Yah's holy Commandments, Judgments and Precepts, the Word will become flesh in us and will produce the fruit of obedience. This obedience will make us blessed, successful and prosperous.

## Yeshua

*Yeshua*—commonly called Jesus Christ—is the real Hebrew name for the Jewish Messiah. In Hebrew, Yeshua means "salvation," "deliverance," and "redemption." Throughout this book, I will use His Hebrew name only.

Yeshua is the Torah made flesh or the Living Torah. As you follow Him and His *Ruach HaKodesh* (Holy Spirit) He will lead you to the truth.

"And you shall know the truth, and the truth shall make you *free*."

John 8:32

*For His glory;*
—**Archbishop Dr. Dominiquae Bierman**

CHAPTER 1

# A Visitation in Chile

*All the nations will be gathered before Him, and He will separate them one from another, as a shepherd divides his sheep from his goats. And He will set the sheep on his right hand, but the goats on the left.*

— MATTHEW 25:32

## ARGENTINA 2001

In late December 2001, Baruch and I personally witnessed the Argentinean Uprising. It seemed as though the whole nation had spilled over onto the streets, protesting the government and the banking system. Hard working people had deposited their money in the banks, but when they needed to withdraw it, the banks had no money to give them. Much of the nation was left cash-less and penniless, and the hearts were boiling. This was a nation in bankruptcy!

We had landed in Argentina only twenty-four hours before this fateful day. As is our custom whenever we arrive in any nation to which we are sent, we blow the shofar at the airport, "the gate" of the nation, or both. Argentina was no exception. Twenty-four hours later, this mass protest exploded. A sea of people of all ages: the young, old, and babies; fathers and mothers with their children all flooded the main streets of Buenos Aires headed to the Presidential Palace – La Casa Rosada, or the Pink House. Our hotel was within walking distance from La Casa Rosada and we witnessed this event right before our eyes. We decided to take our video camera to act as "prophetic journalists" and ventured out into this wave of anger, frustration and solidarity of the Argentinean people. Of course, the hotel staff warned us of the danger of getting ourselves killed in the midst of the mob, but we informed them that we had a special Angelic Escort. With that, we ventured out to an amazing experience.

Later on, the radio reported that several were injured and that most of the supermarkets were being looted by either hungry people, angry people or both. We could also witness when the Presidential helicopter took off from the roof of La Casa Rosada with the president fleeing Argentina. The people had managed to run the president off!

Meanwhile, we were literally trapped in our hotel. All of our meetings for that day had to be cancelled including a pastor's meeting. One dear friend, a pastor and host, asked me half-jokingly in Spanish, my mother tongue, "Dominiquae what on earth did you do when you arrived in Argentina?" to which I replied, "Nothing, I just blew the shofar at the airport of Eseiza."

(This was not, nor would be, the only serious occurrence following my blowing the shofar, the silver trumpet, or both in a nation or a region.)

"Over a million intercessors have been praying for a change of government in Argentina," he added. It was then I connected why Yeshua told me to come to Argentina at this time.

A few weeks earlier, I had called a very good friend of mine, a great lover of Israel, Evangelist Alberto Mottessi, and told him that Yah was sending me to Argentina. He wanted to organize some big meetings there, but I said that my time was short and that I needed to be there in two weeks, which would not give him sufficient time to organize much. Nevertheless, many wonderful pastor friends such as Julio Donati received me well and blessed us. And, God had organized a greater meeting than anyone could have put together - a massive demonstration of all the people of Argentina in every major city and town. We got to blow the shofar before it began, be witnesses while it was going on, and walk the streets of the capital after it had subsided. This is what we saw on the day after the uprising:

Walking on the street that leads to La Casa Rosada we saw many buildings damaged by stones or bullet holes. There were burnt tires strewn here and there and nearly every building had walls or windows damaged. One particular building caught our attention, because it had been damaged far more than any other. This building was riddled with bullet holes and all of its glass completely smashed. It was an imposing building with very dark glass and it seemed that the mob was particularly angry with this building. As we were observing the damage and pondering as to the "why" of this, I noticed police cars next to this building, and then I read the address. I remembered that address: This was none other than the Israeli Embassy of Buenos Aires!

Why would the mob take revenge against the Israeli Embassy for Argentina's financial distress? It immediately brought to mind Nazi Germany in 1933 when Hitler came into power and made the Jews the "scapegoat" for all of Germany's financial problems. After all the events from 1933 through 1945 as well as the occurrences of the terrible Second World War including the atrocious Holocaust which left us Jews bereaved of more than six million, It was clear to me that nothing had changed. The nations were still full of hatred towards the Jews. Given the "right" kind of circumstances, the Jews would be blamed and persecuted again. It did not surprise us when we received the report that The Jewish Agency was organizing a massive Aliyah, immigration to Israel, of Jews from Argentina, *one* day after the mass uprising took place in December of 2001. Since then many, but not enough, Jews have come home to Israel from Argentina.

## CHILE 2001

Baruch and I arrived in my native land of Chile on December 24th, 2001 and nestled ourselves in a hotel in Santiago. We were to minister two days later in Valparaiso near the seaport, plus I was greatly anticipating a reunion with many of my relatives, especially my elderly maternal grandmother.

The 25th of December came, and I rose to pray quite early, however, I ventured out onto the balcony of my room to pray in privacy. What happened next completely caught me off guard. I have had many visitations from the LORD, both dreams and open visions, but I've never heard the LORD so clearly asking me such a serious question before. When Adonai asks a question, it is not because He does not know the answer! So I knew that

He was trying to impart to me a message that I know now has become the major thrust of our ministry.

Preparing to pray, I settled comfortably in a chair looking out from the balcony. The Presence of Yah absorbed me, and I do not even remember the view from that balcony, uncharacteristic of me who never forgets a view! I only remember His question. It resonated into my entire being:

"Dominiquae, what would happen if I came back right now? How many nations would be Sheep Nations?"

"You see," He said, "I will judge the nations by these two standards:

1. My eternal, unchanging righteous Law
2. By how the nations treat My Jewish people

He had my attention! Rapidly, passages of Scripture ran through my mind. One was Matthew 25:32: *He will gather the nations and will separate them as the sheep from the goats.* I considered many other verses. It did not take but a second for me to say, "none Lord."

As He was talking, my spirit, mind and heart were racing at the speed of light. It was like the whole Bible was opening before me with a new understanding and clarity about the condition of the world and of the nations, one like I had never had before! This was a visitation from Yah, the Almighty was manifesting His will to His soldier and I was listening.

"I gave My disciples the commission to disciple the nations, all the ethnic groups of the earth, and to teach them My Commandments. I said to make disciples of all nations and yet after 2000 years of My gospel being on earth, you cannot present to Me one Sheep Nation!"

I knew that He was right. Not one nation had adopted Yahveh's Commandments as their constitution. Neither was there any nation that I knew of that was guiltless concerning Israel. In 1938, a time when Hitler had already begun His plan to rid the world of its Jews, an international convention met in Evian, France to discuss the "Jewish Problem." Not one nation was willing to give shelter to even some of the Jews from Germany and Europe, in order to rescue them from Hitler's claws (except the Dominican Republic who was willing to take a few of those who knew agriculture).

**For I was hungry and you gave me no food; I was thirsty and you gave me no drink; I was a stranger and you did not take me in, naked and you did not clothe Me, sick and in prison (in concentration camps and ghettos!) and you did not visit Me... Assuredly I say to you, inasmuch as you did not do it to the least of these you did not do it to Me.**

Matthew 25:42–45

All nations knew what was happening. US bombers flew over Auschwitz countless times. They could have bombed the death camps of Birkenau, but did not. England knew. The church knew, but not one denomination arose to oppose Hitler or the Holocaust.

We took a tour to Auschwitz in March 2003, and were shocked by a new exhibition on display. This exhibition consisted of documents and pictures detailing how the church of its time, both Catholic and Protestant, had given Hitler their blessing as he entered into government. Later on, not one church group or organization stood up to oppose him!

Here and there, individuals such as Corrie Ten Boom and Oscar Schindler stood bravely for what was right, but by far they were the minority. They were not part of any church or national effort; they were acting on their own.

I was beginning to get the picture. If Yeshua returned that day (Christmas day 2001) *all* the nations, including the USA, Switzerland, Australia, Italy, Chile, Argentina, et cetera, would be judged as goat nations.

**Then He will say to those in the left hand, "Depart from Me you cursed, into the everlasting are prepared for the devil and his angels."**

Matthew 25:41

In other words all the nations of the earth are under a curse!

**I will bless those who bless you, and I will curse him who curses you; and in you all the families of the earth will be blessed *(if* they bless you!).**

Genesis 12:3

More Scriptures began to come to mind as the Holy Spirit, the Ruach HaKodesh, was leading me into the understanding of Yahveh's message. He took me to Isaiah 34:1–8.

**Come near, you nations, to hear; and heed you people! Let the earth hear. And all that is in it, the world and all things that come forth from it.**

Isaiah 34:1–8

I was 'earth,' and I was listening!

**For the indignation of the LORD is against all nations, and his fury against all their armies; He has utterly destroyed them, He has given them over to the slaughter.**

Isaiah 34:2

This is in past tense, which means that Yahveh has already done it in His mind. It is a 'done deal,' and ready to be manifested in the natural.

There are no speculations here; the LORD has already decided to destroy all the nations, not one Sheep Nation insight!

**Also their slain shall be thrown out, their stench shall rise from their corpses, and the mountains shall be melted with their blood. All the host of heaven shall be dissolved... For it is the day of the LORD's vengeance, the year of recompense for the cause of Zion.**

Isiah 34:3-4, 8

Yahveh has spoken and Yahveh will do it.

I was trembling before the LORD as He kept on speaking to me, "Dominiquae, the devil has always wanted to destroy Israel, and through Israel, also to cause Me to judge all the nations. Satan is not only desirous to annihilate Israel, but the whole human race. His plan has been to cause people to hate My Torah, My righteous Laws and My people, the Jews. I called the ecclesia, My called-out ones, to teach the nations to love My holy Commandments and to love all peoples, especially the Jews, My chosen ones."

I broke before My Father, the judge of the universe who is love and said, "Father, we the church have failed to teach the nations and to make disciples of all nations. After 2,000 years of 'gospel,' we have miserably failed the Great Commission. We, the church, have not done the job."

"The church has done the job," the LORD said to me in a very arm tone, "but she has done the job wrongly. The church has used her authority to teach the nations to hate My Law and to hate My Jews."

My mind was spinning and my heart racing. Truly, historically speaking, every horrendous massacre of Jews from the second century and on has been carried out by the church, in the name of Christ, and due to anti-Semitic Christian doctrine. No one can refute, without making a fool of himself, that for the last 1,800 years, particularly the last 1,600 years since the infamous 'Council of Nicaea,' the Christian church has been the worst persecutor the Jewish people have ever known.

I have always felt surprised and distressed that Bible schools and seminaries do not teach this 'bloody history.' All the 'Church History' books completely ignore the persecution of the Jews, which has been one of the most prevalent marks of the Christian Religion since it was officially instituted by Emperor Constantine and the Gentile church fathers in AD 325. Christian events such as the Spanish Inquisition, the pogroms, the Crusades and the Holocaust are not studied in any Christian Bible school. If they are mentioned at all, they are treated lightly and quickly.

But it was that day, Christmas day 2001, that the LORD visited me in Chile, one of the most anti-Semitic nations in the world; a country where "the Holy Office," the institution of the Spanish Inquisition, still exists. A country that has given shelter to many officers of the Nazi regime who are in hiding. It was there that the Almighty was visiting me and literally telling me that the whole world was going to hell! And that the wrong teachings of the Christian church were sending them there!

He did not say, "Go into all the world and teach Christianity to the nations. Turn them into pagans and teach them how to celebrate the false deities Tammuz and Ishtar during the foreign celebrations of Christmas and Easter." He did not say, "Go to the nations and tell them that My Laws are done away with, and that they are free from My Laws." He did not tell them, "Go into all the nations and tell them that the Jews killed Christ so they deserve to be second class citizens and live in hell forever as their Gentile church fathers such as John Chrisostom and St. Augustine had told them." And He did not tell them to, "go and tell the nations to get rid of the Jews because they are 'vermin' and 'plague,' such as their father Martin Luther had told them..."

No, no, no! The Great Commission was given to His Jewish apostles that were not Christian and knew nothing about Christianity. They were His disciples, His followers, and He had taught them Torah. They had celebrated the biblical holy days with Him. They had eaten 'Kosher' and clean food with Him. This is what He purposefully told His Jewish Disciples:

**All authority has been given unto Me in heaven and on earth. Go therefore and make disciples of all nations. Teaching them to observe (to do!) all things that I have commanded you; and lo, I am with you always and even to the end of the age.**

Matthew 28:18–20

I wept before the God of Heaven, ELOHIM the Creator, and began to repent on behalf of the church.

"LORD forgive us! Please give us more time that we might teach the nations Your Commandments and Your love for Israel."

I borrowed time from the God of Israel on that Christmas day of 2001 in my native land of Chile. And since then, my dear people, we are running on borrowed time.

In my book, *The Healing Power of the Roots*, First printed in 1996, I said that the Lord had told me that teaching the Jewish roots to the church was a matter of life and death as: the church had been like a beautiful rose cut off from her garden (Israel, the Jews and the Torah) and put in a vase for two days. But if it's not replanted back in the original garden, on the third day, it will die. Since I wrote that book, we have already entered into the Third Day, The Third Millennium…

And now Yahveh has visited me about the nations.

Preaching the Good News of Yeshua, the Jewish Messiah, teaching Yahveh's Torah, and teaching the nations to love Him and His Jewish people is a Matter of life and death to ALL the nations of the earth!

**And it shall happen in that day that I will make Jerusalem a very heavy stone for all peoples; all who would heave it away will surely be cut in pieces, though all nations of the earth are gathered against it… It shall be on that day that I will seek to destroy all nations that come against Jerusalem**

Zechariah 12:3,12

> "Close your eyes for a moment and feel the pulsating rhythm of the 'Hate-The-Jew' song as it captivates the nations of the world. The Muslims are dancing to its beat. Communist China is familiar with its tune. Europe often moves to its tempo. Some Americans are humming along. The 'church' has written the lyrics. And Satan is orchestrating it all!" (Brown)

CHAPTER 2

# Give Me Sheep Nations!

*Ask of Me and I will give you the nations for your inheritance,
and the ends of the earth for your possession.*

— Psalms 2:8

This has been my heart cry since I can remember, but all the more since the Lord's visitation in Chile. I carry with me a passion to see entire nations turned to Him!

There have been many books written by very well-informed preachers and teachers concerning, 'taking cities for God' or 'spiritual mapping' et cetera, but I believe that in these End times, the outpouring of Yah's glory will be on entire nations.

The Greek word for nations is *ethnos*, which means "ethnic or racial groups."

There is no better spiritual strategy concerning each nation than to lead that nation or ethnic group into repentance for sins of omission (what they did not do to help) or sins of commission (what they did do to harm) against the Jews and the Nation of

Israel. That whole theme covers the entire Bible. There is no way to miss Yah's blessing on the nations if we deal with it correctly. But of course an unrepentant church cannot lead any nation into repentance. It must begin with us!

We cannot teach the nations to obey Yah's Commandments if we disobey them and teach others to do so. Neither can we teach the nations to love Israel if we do not love her in action if we still harbor anti-Semitism in our hearts. However, a repentant humbled church, a true ecclesia, *will* lead the nations into repentance. I am believing Yah to give me a few nations to bring before His throne.

The God of Israel is not a loser! He sent His Son to the world, so that the world might be saved. He is not going to hand all these nations to the devil on a silver platter. He is shaking us up like He did Jonah:

- He is correcting our course and giving us 'New Bible Training'
- He has allowed some of us to be in the belly of the big fish of trials for a while
- He has readied others with a fervent message that will turn nations around!

There is nothing wrong with a message of 'turn or burn,' since this is what He says in His Word. Is He not the God of Absolutes? In fact that message of 'turn or burn' that Jonah preached caused repentance and salvation in an entire nation!

The reason why Yah was about to destroy Nineveh was the same reason why He is about to destroy all the nations in this present hour:

- They had broken His Commandments
- They had plundered Israel

Nineveh was the capital of Assyria, and during the 8th century BC Assyria had destroyed and taken captive the

Northern Kingdom of Israel, which are commonly known as 'the ten lost tribes.' The Assyrians preceded Hitler by thousands of years. They completely dismantled and dismembered the tribes and the families and scattered them throughout the Assyrian Empire (which covered all the known world at that time), so that they could not be a people any more. Today we find traces of them in some temples in Japan, among the Indians in India, among the Nigerians, the Ghanans, and many more. Some of them circumcise their boys on the 8th day and do not know why. Others light candles and prepare a festive meal on Friday night and do not know why. Others have Hebrew words and Hebrew symbols in their language and culture and do not know why.

The same thing happened when the Jews were persecuted during the Spanish Inquisition. Many pretended to be Catholic in order to escape burning in the Fires of The Inquisition, and yet kept Jewish traditions in secret. Today they are called "The Conversos" or the "Crypto Jews." There are millions of them all over the world.

When Jonah came on the scene, the ten tribes had disappeared, and Israel had dwindled into a very small nation because of the captivity. Jonah understandably hated the Assyrians and especially their capital Nineveh. It was the most wicked city on the face of the earth. They were like Berlin, Germany, the seat of power that ordered the extermination of six million Jews during the Holocaust.

Jonah escaped His calling and took a different ship, because he did not want the compassion of Yah to be poured out on these wicked murderers. He knew that when the Almighty gives a message of judgment before He actually does it, it is because He is giving one more chance for repentance. Notice that when

He sent the angels to destroy Sodom. He did not announce it beforehand, neither did He allow for any time... there was no place for mercy!

Nineveh was a different case scenario, as Jonah came announcing the judgment:

> **So Jonah arose and went to Nineveh, according to the Word of the LORD. Now Nineveh was an exceedingly great city, a three days journey in extent. And Jonah began to enter the city on the first day's walk. Then he cried out and said, "Yet forty days and Nineveh shall be overthrown!" So the people of Nineveh believed God, proclaimed a fast, and put on sackcloth, from the greatest to the least of them. Then word came to the king of Nineveh; and he arose from his throne and laid aside his robe, covered himself with sackcloth and sat in ashes... Then God saw their works, that they turned from their evil ways; and God relented from the disaster that He had said He would bring upon them, and He did not do it.**
>
> **Jonah 3:3–10**

In other words, because of their faith, that caused them to repent in dust and ashes, the LORD also repented from the evil that He had already decreed.

I believe that as we obey Yah and preach repentance to the nations, many will fall on their knees before Him. Even wicked nations such as Germany, Poland, and Switzerland that were involved in plundering the Jews will have a chance.

**And should I not pity Nineveh, that great city in which are more than one hundred and twenty thousand persons who**

cannot discern between their right hand and their left and much livestock?

Jonah 4:11

But before we can preach repentance to the nations, we need to apologize...

CHAPTER 3

# The Church Must Repent First

*For the time has come for judgment to begin at the house of God; and if it begins with us first, what will be the end of those who do not obey the gospel of God?*

— 1 PETER 4:17

The Lutheran church right across the street from the Birkenau death camps in Auschwitz. The SS officers and the Nazi soldiers, all baptized Protestant Christians, went to services on Sundays with their wives and children after over 10,000 Jews a day. One and a half million Jews alone were exterminated in Auschwitz by these Christians.

> 'Many Christians when confronted with the Shoa (Holocaust) gaze on it as if some aliens landed on earth, took on the name 'Nazi,' and proceeded to torture Jews. They regard the perpetrators of these monstrous acts as

from another planet, as people who otherwise did not hug their children, weep at the death of a parent, bleed when they were wounded – in other words non-human creatures without a conscience, automatons of some mad and evil creator. But the Shoa is not the story about a group of alien people, rather about human beings. And they, we must admit, were primarily Christians – from the great Lutheran and Catholic traditions. Somehow they had lost that which made them followers of Jesus or they had chosen to suppress it in their horrid pursuit of killing Jews. For some, to think of Christian participation in the Shoa is so horrific that it must be immediately denied. They protest quickly that the perpetrators were not Christian, for, they reason, a Christian by definition could not have committed such barbarity, such obscenity. But then there were all those who were bystanders. True, they didn't pull the trigger or herd Jews into boxcars. Rather they were on the sidelines, knowing or half-suspecting what was happening to their Jewish neighbors. And the bystanders were Christians." (Ritner, Smith and Steinfeldt)

Yahveh has already decreed evil upon all the nations of the earth. As with Nineveh, because of His compassion, He is announcing that His judgment is about to come to *all* nations. However, the Word says that He *must* judge His house first, so the church will be judged first. And, it will be judged for the exact same things:

- For breaking and teaching others to break Yah's Torah and holy Commandments in the guise of a perverted licentious 'gospel' that has created a lukewarm church with no power.

It is a 'gospel' that is totally disconnected from the original Jewish/apostolic roots of the church.
- For hating the Jews, teaching 'replacement theology,' calling every Torah teacher a 'Judaizer' and for not helping the Jews during their intense need at the time of the Holocaust and now at the time of their national struggle for freedom from terror.

Yahveh cannot judge the nations until He deals with His own. Does He want to judge? Hardly! But He is announcing it so that there can be time for repentance!

No doubt that there are some individuals and even leaders in the church that do not deserve this judgment, but He is looking at the church as a whole. He will, however, deal with each group separately as He does in the Book of Revelation chapters two and three.

At such a late hour in the "ticking" biblical clock there are some well-respected prophets and leaders reviving anti-Semitic theologies. These ideas are spreading once again in a most violent way throughout the body of Messiah. One of them, a leader of an entire movement, has implied and excused the atrocities perpetrated in the name of Christ through Christianity against the Jewish people as "a need of the church to define herself apart from her spiritual parents, in order to have her 'unique identity' and basically 'rescue' the New Covenant from falling in the hands of 'Judaizers.'" The following is an exact quote, and it reminds me of some of Martin Luther or Constantine's remarks. Except, it's neither of them, nor a ghost from the past, but one of the most respected leaders of the charismatic – prophetic movement worldwide:

"In this storyline of the Bible, the Father married Israel and together they had a Son. The Son was also to have a bride -- the church. From the very beginning the mother, Israel, tried to impose herself on the young bride of Christ through the 'Judaizers' who tried to bring her under the yoke of the Law. This was an attempt to make the young church completely co-dependent and swallow up her unique identity. If this had happened, there would have been no New Covenant, and eventually all of the truth of the Messiah would have been swallowed up. There had to be a separation – a leaving until the church was able to establish her own identity with Christ, her Husband."

In my book *The Healing Power of The Roots*, you will find more about what this 'separation' has brought forth. Also, please see in this book the appendix called "Two Weddings and a Divorce" for more on the 'fruit' of that separation.

Let me identify several common errors mentioned in the quoted article:

- The word Judaizers is not found in the Bible. It is, rather, anti-Semitic terminology used by many of the Gentile church fathers in order to humiliate the Jewish disciples at the end of the first century when the number of Gentile disciples began to outgrow the number of Jewish disciples.
- The young 'bride of Christ' mentioned here is only the Gentile portion of the church, since the Jewish portion had already been banished at the time of the Nicene Creed when Emperor Constantine said: "Therefore we ought not to have anything in common with the Jews, for the Savior has shown us another way. Therefore we desire to separate ourselves from the detestable company of the Jews."

- The *true* bride of Messiah is depicted in Revelation 21 and has 12 gates that are the 12 tribes of Israel and 12 foundations, which are the 12 Jewish apostles of the Lamb.
- The unique identity of the church is not as a Gentile Christian.
- Her unique identity comes from her being grafted into the Olive tree, which is Israel. (Romans 11)
- The New Covenant was not given to the Gentiles nor to a Gentile church, but rather to the Jews. As a matter of fact, there is no New or Renewed Covenant without the Jews. Yah only made a covenant with Israel, and Gentiles can join in through faith. (Jeremiah 31:31–34). So separation from the Jews cannot 'safe keep' the New Covenant that does not exist without the Jews.

The author of the quoted article is in great error as are most of his followers and like major portions of the church today that believe similarly. Look at this quote from the same person:

"There is much controversy today about what is referred to as 'replacement theology.' This is the theology whereby the church completely replaces Israel in God's plan, and all of the promises that were given to Israel are really meant for the church. This is to some degree a reaction to Israel's attempts to destroy the unique identity of the church, so the church has also gone through a long period, centuries, of trying to destroy the unique identity of Israel. Now, possibly in reaction to the replacement theology, there are "counter-replacement" theologies being promoted whereby Israel completely displaces the church in God's plan at the end. Both of these theologies are in error, and disregard major portions of Scripture in both the Old and New Testaments."

Replacement theology has been the theology behind all the murders carried out during the Spanish Inquisition and the Nazi Holocaust. This respected preacher says that replacement theology is a *reaction* of the church. Can you call the massacre of millions of Jews in the name of Christianity a "reaction to preserve her unique identity"? And if so, what kind of identity does this church have that its reaction is *murder!*? I believe that this particular preacher, as well as most in the church, has a severe case of misplaced identity.

Hitler said that he was only following Martin Luther's instructions. Let us take a look at them. The following excerpt is from *Our Hands are Stained with Blood* by Michael Brown where he quotes directly from Martin Luther's writings. This was written by Luther after he was frustrated from trying to evangelize the Jews and when he was old and sick.

> "What shall we Christians do with this damned rejected race of Jews? First their synagogues should be set on free. Secondly their homes should likewise be broken down and destroyed. Thirdly they should be deprived of their prayer books and Talmuds. Fourthly their rabbis must be forbidden under threat of death to teach anymore. Fifthly passports and traveling privileges should be absolutely forbidden to the Jews... To sum up dear princes and nobles, who have Jews in your domains, if this advice of mine does not suit you, then find a better one. So that you and we may all be free of this insufferable, devilish burden – the Jews." (Brown)

Hitler followed Luther's instructions meticulously and quoted him while doing so. The fruit? Over six million Jews exterminated in horrendous death camps and gas chambers, and many survivors scarred for life.

Because of rejecting the Jews and the Torah, the instructions of Yah in righteousness, the church today has a terrible lack of holiness, integrity and righteous standards. The rate of divorce within the church and without is almost the same percentage, as is the rate of abortions, child abuse and wife abuse. The difference is that in the church, things are kept quiet and disguised under a false spiritual façade.

I was once in a Far Eastern nation and preaching within a spirit-filled denomination that was going through revival. Many of the women were trying desperately to receive counseling from me. As the pastor permitted it, many came to me to confess that their husbands were abusing them: sexually and otherwise, and that the only thing the pastor had to say about it was that "they needed to submit no matter what."

I cannot mention how many ministers suffer from lust, commit violent adultery and fornication and yet, we are still asleep and refuse to see that something is seriously wrong. We cannot preach against Yah's Laws and standards of righteousness and still be blessed.

**He that turns away his ear from hearing the Law, even his prayer shall be an abomination.**

Proverbs 28:9

"Many will say to Me in that day, 'Lord, Lord, have we not prophesied in Your name, cast out demons in Your name, and done many wonders in Your name?' And then I will declare to them, 'I never knew you; depart from Me, you who practice Lawlessness!'"

Matthew 7:22–23

Another word for 'workers of iniquity' is those that are Lawless and do not want to accept my Laws and Commandments. Yes, you prophesy and cast out devils and desire to do work signs and wonders, yet you reject my Law. Many well-meaning believers really want to serve the holy God of Israel but they have been told so many times that the Law is not for today, that they are in confusion. Their intentions may be good, but the holy God of Israel sees them as 'workers of iniquity.'

One day the LORD showed me a vision. He showed me that, immediately, when a person repents and accepts Him as LORD and Messiah, because of His blood, they are instantly carried into the Holy of Holies. As they come before Him in the Holy of Holies, they found there the Ark of the Covenant and inside the Ark, the three elements: (Hebrews 9:4)

- The Two Tablets of the Testimony – the Torah or the Law
- The Jar of Manna – representing Yah's grace and provision
- The Rod of Aaron that budded – representing the authority of the priesthood

Most of the time a new believer, upon arrival in the church, is immediately indoctrinated with God loves him, that He is not mad at him because he is now free from the bondage to the Law, and that the Law was given to the Jews and it is not for today anymore. So this new believer meets the Ark of the Covenant and he meets with the two 'Tablets of the Law' and rejects them because of false Christian doctrines. Immediately he is thrown out of the Holy of Holies and into the Outer Court, where he begins again the journey from being a sinner to 'being a saint.' He goes into a vicious cycle of sin and defeat, which never allows for the true mark of the New Covenant to be upon him.

What is that true mark?

The Torah or Law of Yahveh written on our hearts and in our minds:

> Behold the days are coming says Yahveh, when I will make a New Covenant with the house of Israel and with the house of Judah. Not according to the covenant that I made with their fathers... But this is the covenant that I will make with the house of Israel after those days says Yahveh; I will put my Law in their minds and write it on their hearts; and I will be their ELOHIM and they shall be my people.
>
> Jeremiah 31:31–33

Please notice that the New or Renewed Covenant is not made with the Gentiles but with Judah and Israel. The Gentiles have entrance to the New Covenant through the Jewish Messiah as they JOIN with their Jewish brethren in the New Covenant. There is no such thing as the Gentile church. The church is, all of it, grafted into Israel. There is not a 'unique Gentile church' and a 'unique Jewish church.' There is only *one* ecclesia/church and it is grafted into the Olive tree. (Please read all of Romans 11 and Revelation 21.) The church needs to return to its *original identity!*

And though each nation carries a unique identity and calling, the focal point and the foundational Laws have to be the same: the same Yah, the same Word and Torah, the same Spirit, the same allegiance to the people of Israel. (See more about this point in the chapter "The Key of Abraham.")

## PROPHETIC INVITATION TO YOU

"Come let us go up to the mountain of the LORD, to the house of the God of Jacob; He will teach us His ways, and we shall walk in His path." For out of Zion shall go forth the Law and the Word of Yahveh from Jerusalem.

Isaiah 2:3

No holiness, no power, no SHEEP NATIONS!

CHAPTER 4

# The Heavenly Constitution

*Now it shall come to pass in the latter days that the mountain of the LORD's House shall be established on the top of the mountains and shall be exalted above the hills and peoples shall follow to it. Many nations shall come and say, "Come, and let us go up to the mountain of the LORD, to the house of the God of Jacob. He will teach us His ways, and we shall walk in His paths." For out of Zion the Law shall go forth and the Word of the LORD from Jerusalem,*

— MICAH 4:1–2

It is obvious from this passage of Scripture and from a similar one in Isaiah 2, that it is Yahveh's will that the nations learn Torah. The only way to change the nations from goat nations to sheep nations is by fulfilling the Great Commission and by teaching God's Commandments to the nations. It is also clear that the Law of the LORD does not come out of America or Europe, not even out of Argentina or Singapore, but rather out of Zion, out of Jerusalem, Israel and the Jewish people. His plan has never changed and so in these End times, the original plan is being restored. The LORD is rising up some redeemed Jews that know their covenants, both the Abrahamic Covenant and the Messianic Covenant through Yeshua, and they are being sent in an apostolic prophetic way to teach Torah and Yah's Laws to the nations.

I believe that as the church begins to pray for them, support them, and recognize them, they will have the anointing and the power to turn *entire nations to Yah.*

**Thus says the LORD of Hosts: "In those days ten men from every language of the nations shall grasp the fringes of the garment of a Jew saying, 'Let us go with you, for we have heard that God is with you.'"**

Zechariah 8:23

In some translations it says *sleeve,* instead of *'fringes,'* but the real word is *fringes,* sometimes translated as *"wings."* Every Torah observant Jew has some special tassels on the four corners of his garment. This is to obey the Commandment written in Numbers 15:37–40:

**Again the LORD spoke to Moses, saying, "Speak to the children of Israel. Tell them to make tassels on the corners of their garments throughout their generations, and to put a blue thread in the tassels of the corners. And you shall have the tassel, that you may look upon it and remember all the Commandments of the LORD and do them, and that you may not follow the harlotry to which your own heart and your**

own eyes are inclined. And that you may remember and do all my Commandments, and be holy for your ELOHIM."

Numbers 15:37–40

The fact that ten men of every language of the nations will grasp a Torah observant Jew from these tassels, which represent the Commandments, is very meaningful. In other words, there will be a move and already is. A God-ordained move among all the different ethnic groups in the nations to learn Torah from some Torah observant Jews. I believe that these are Messianic Jews, believers in Yeshua, that also keep the Commandments of Yah.

**And the dragon (Satan) was enraged with the woman (Israel), and he went to make war with the rest of her offspring, who keep the Commandments of God and have the testimony of Yeshua the Messiah.**

Revelation 12:17

By *Torah Observant*, I do not mean *religious and orthodox Jews*, (though some of them will be from that background and there is nothing wrong with that). I mean born again, anointed Jewish men and women, who are full of the Holy Spirit, power and wisdom, and who walk in obedience to Yahveh's Commandments as revealed to them by the Holy Spirit.

They will and are walking in a Spirit of Revelation for the purpose of restoration of Torah and truth to the nations. You will know that you are in the presence of one of them because of the glory that they carry. The combination of anointing and character will be obvious. They will combine the fine balance between the Gifts of the Spirit and the Fruit of the Spirit. (See 1 Corinthians 12 and Galatians 5:21–22).

*Please do not follow anyone that tells you they are 'Torah Observant' and yet there is no holiness or anointing in their lives!* When one begins to obey the Law of the LORD by the power of the Holy Spirit and He writes it in our hearts, we will begin to see and to do mighty works like the apostles of old. Remember that this is an apostolic move, and it brings:

## TRUTH, FREEDOM, AND RESTORATION

Since the times of the Early church and until now, the dragon has been fighting against Torah observant Messianic Jews. At the time of the infamous Council of Nicaea, the devil used the Gentile portion of the church to get rid of their Messianic Jewish brothers and sisters altogether and set up an alternative 'church system' called Christianity. At the beginning, the believers were called "The Followers of the Way" or "Disciples of Yeshua." It seemed to be that the Jewish believers disappeared altogether from the scene of history. They underwent much persecution from their Christian 'brothers' from the second century onwards. From then until now, the Messianic believers that have believed in a gospel with Torah and Spirit were and are still misunderstood and are persecuted by modern day 'prophets' and 'theologians' who are still calling them 'Judaizers.' However, Yah said that these will be the ones that mankind, from *every tribe and tongue*, will follow in these End times, and He never lies.

Why ten men of every language of the nations?

The number ten for people is mentioned in one particular instance in the Scriptures, when Abraham was negotiating with Yah about the salvation of Sodom and Gomorra. Ten was *the minimal number stipulated by God in order to refrain from destroying these cities.*

**Then he said, "Let not the L**ORD **be angry, and I will speak but once more: Suppose ten should be found there?" So He said, "I will not destroy it for the sake of ten."**

**Genesis 18**

Also it takes ten men (called a *minian*) to start a prayer service in any synagogue and to learn Torah.

In the same way Adonai is looking for at least ten people from every language and ethnic group that will be willing to learn His Commandments and follow the Jews that follow the Messiah of Israel and His Word. Those ten are a minimal group that will be able to stand for their language group to be saved as a people. Through this minimum group of 'Ten Righteous,' entire ethnic groups will become, "*Sheep ethnos.*"

As the nations begin to learn Torah from these modern day, male and female Jewish apostles, entire nations will begin to shift into position for salvation. Entire nations or ethnic groups, will begin to choose Yahveh's Ten Commandments as their Ethnic group's *Constitution*.

It is the word of the constitution that shapes a nation and anyone that opposes the constitution or breaks one of its laws becomes the enemy of that nation.

I am expecting many nations to replace their present day constitutions for the Ten Commandments. I will call the Ten Commandments: "The Heavenly Constitution."

# The Heavenly Constitution

> For what great nation is there that has ELOHIM so near to it, as Yahveh our ELOHIM is to us, for whatever reason we may call upon Him? And what great nation is there that has such statutes and righteous judgments as are in all this Law which I set before you this day?
>
> Deuteronomy 4:8

When the Torah was given to Israel, it transformed Israel into the greatest nation on the face of the earth. Until then, they were a nation of slaves with great promises, but after Mount Sinai, they became a great nation to reckon with. In the light of this we can better understand Yeshua's words to His Jewish disciples in Matthew 5.

> Do not think that I came to destroy the Law or the prophets (by misinterpretation), I did not come to destroy but to fulfill (interpret it to the full). For assuredly I say to you, till heaven and earth pass away, one jot or one title will by no means pass from the Law till all is fulfilled. Whoever therefore breaks one of the least of these (Torah) Commandments and teaches men so, shall be called least in the kingdom of heaven; but whoever does and teaches them, he shall be called great in the kingdom of heaven.
>
> Matthew 5:17–20

In other words, Yeshua was saying that He did not come to destroy the Constitution given by Yah through Moses, He did not come as an enemy of the nation, but rather *He came as a legislator to bring forth the Constitution to its full meaning and potential.*

He was now saying that we needed to teach the principles of this Constitution to others, and in Matthew 28:19, He repeats it by saying: *"Go and make disciples of all nations... Teaching them to obey all that I have commanded you."* Go and teach them to be obedient to My Constitution for all nations, My Torah, the same one that My Father gave that I have interpreted to you so that you can go and establish all the nations in it. That is the Great Commission! We are sent by the Legislator of the Universe to restore the DNA of the nations, the Heavenly Constitution. The Torah, the Word that rules and shapes the nations into the greatness that Yahveh intended for them. "In you, Abraham, in your God, in your Torah and your descendants' Torah, all the families, Ethnos, nations of the earth will be blessed and will be restored to the full potential for which they were created and then My salvation will come."

When we teach Yahveh's Commandments we open the door of greatness to the nations, and what we sow, we also reap. As we lead people to greatness we become great ourselves!

**Listen to Me, My people; and give ear to Me O My nation: For Law will proceed from Me, and I will make My justice rest as a light of the peoples. My righteousness is near, My salvation has gone forth, and My arms will judge the peoples, the coastlands will wait upon Me and on My arm they will trust.**

Isaiah 51:4–5

I want you to see the connection between the Law that proceeds from Yah to the nations and His salvation, Yeshua. First the nations learn His Law, His Torah. They trust in Him and establish His Torah as the nation's constitution, and then comes His salvation. That was the way that salvation came to the Gentiles for the first time.

The first Gentile believer was a God-fearing Gentile named Cornelius. He loved the Jews, prayed and gave alms to them. He was a Torah-keeping, synagogue-attending Gentile. He already honored Yah's Laws, and therefore, when Peter preached the Good News of Messiah to him, the Holy Spirit fell on him and his household, and they all received water baptism that day! (Acts 10)

In fact, all the first Gentiles that received salvation, were Torah- keeping, synagogue-going, God-fearing Gentiles. Their knowledge of Torah helped them to get ready for the gospel. The problem began when pagan Gentiles began to turn to the LORD, and that is why the Acts 15 apostolic meeting took place. It would have been unheard of to say to Cornelius after his water baptism, *"Well now Cornelius, since you are born again, you are free from the Torah, you can break the Shabbat and eat pork if you would like."* This Yah-fearing, righteous Gentile would have thought that you were out of your mind and a heretic, and he would have been right!

That is why in Acts 15, Gentiles leaving paganism and turning to Yah were given only four Torah instructions. They were then sent to the synagogues where the Torah was being preached so they could learn how to turn from the rest of their pagan practices.

**Therefore I judge that we should not trouble those from among the Gentiles who are turning to God... for Moses has**

**had throughout many generations those who preach him in every city, being read in the synagogues every Shabbat.**

Acts 15:19–21

In other words, dear Gentiles, come into the kingdom, separate yourselves from immorality, idolatry and profanity, and go on Shabbat to the synagogues to listen to the rest of the Law of the LORD!

Today I would say to every Gentile turning to Yah to find himself a place of worship where they teach Torah, the Word of Faith and move in the power of the Holy Spirit. Those are Messianic, apostolic, prophetic centers of worship that are rising up in these End of Times. Just like when Yahveh was restoring the baptism in the Holy Spirit and praying in other tongues, we used to advise people to get into a 'spirit-filled church' because that was how the LORD was moving in His church.

Afterwards, the LORD began to restore faith in His goodness and in His Word for healing and provision, so we sent people to 'spirit-filled, Word of Faith' kinds of churches.

Today a spirit-filled, Word of Faith church is not enough. It needs to be spirit-filled and open to being instructed in the Torah of the LORD and in the LORD's righteous standards. I am not talking about any Rabbinical or religious traditions but rather about the Law of Yahveh in His holy Word. Most of the time, there will be a need to be connected to some apostolic Messianic Jews for that purpose. (Not all Messianic Jews are apostolic or have this revelation.)

The LORD is restoring to the Torah observant, empowered, and prophetic Messianic Jews their rightful apostolic place within the body of Messiah and the nations.

Listen to me, you who know righteousness, you people in whose heart is my Law (born again, spirit-filled, New Covenant people, see Jeremiah 31:31-34); do not fear the reproach of men nor be afraid of their insults. For the moth will eat them up as a garment, and the worm will eat them up as wool; but my righteousness will be forever, and my salvation from generation to generation.

Isaiah 51:7–8

## CHAPTER 5

# The Key of Abraham

*Now the L*ORD *had said to Abram: 'Get out of your country, from your family and from your father's house, to a land that I will show you. I will make you a great nation; I will bless you and make your name great; and you shall be a blessing. I will bless those who bless you and I will curse him who curses you. And in you all the families of the earth will be blessed.*
— GENESIS 12:1–3

The entire plan of Yah for the redemption of mankind flows through one man – Abraham, who was a former idol worshipper from Arabia, but who was called to follow the Creator into an unknown land and an unknown faith. By then man had fallen away so far from the Creator that no one knew how to worship Him anymore, neither did they know Him or His ways. So what happened to Abram, the idol worshipper, was a tremendous revolution that took tremendous resolve on his part to obey.

> And Abraham believed Yah, and it counted to him for righteousness.
>
> Genesis 15:6

Abram believed an unseen, invisible God and exchanged his tangible idols to follow Him. His faith produced the fruit of obedience to His instructions as true faith always does. Faith that is not followed by obedience to Yah is not real, and it will not bring any blessing.

As Abram would proceed to follow ELOHIM's instructions, he would be inheriting an amazingly great inheritance for all the generations to come! The obedience of this one man would cause the whole world to be redeemed from the curse of The Fall. Just as the disobedience of one man – Adam led the whole world into the curse, the obedience of one man – Abraham, would engage the Creator into restoring the lost blessing to mankind. Had Abraham refused to go with Yah and follow him to an unknown land and an unknown faith, there would be no New Covenant today.

It is very sobering as we meditate on this, to understand that our obedience to Yah's instructions, Torah, Commandments, which is a product of true faith, can have such an amazing impact! But think about this: Our disobedience has an equally negative impact, just as the disobedience of Adam did! We are created in the very image of ELOHIM, and what we do carries enormous weight and consequences. That is why Satan has sought to lead man into disobedience since the beginning. That is why the devil himself has caused the church to fall into deception by hating Yahveh's Commandments, by hating the Jews and by misinterpretations of the Scriptures. The purpose of this old snake is to keep the children of Yah in defeat through sin and disobedience, Torahless and Lawlessness, because it carries enormous consequences. Not just to them, but to all of mankind. One of us in obedience can and will change entire nations in Yeshua's name!

The unknown land, to which Yah led Abram, later known as Abraham, was called Canaan, and eventually it was called Israel. Israel is also the name of the grandson of Abraham, who bore Isaac, who bore Jacob, whose name changed to Israel. Israel bore 12 sons and a daughter, and later his 12 sons were called the Twelve Tribes of Israel.

The Land of Israel was promised to Abraham and to his descendants forever. Its boundaries were from the Nile River in Egypt to the Euphrates River in Iraq.

**On the same day the LORD made a covenant with Abram, saying: "To your descendants I have given this land, from the river of Egypt to the great river, the River Euphrates."**

Genesis 15:18 (see also Deuteronomy 1:7–8)

In the midst of that land, during the time of King David, an ancient city was chosen to become the seat of the government of the Nation of Israel and also the Throne of the LORD.

**At that time Jerusalem shall be called the throne of the LORD, and all the nations shall be gathered to it, to the name of Yahveh, to Jerusalem. No more shall they follow the dictates of their evil hearts.**

Jeremiah 3:17

That city was then and is still called Jerusalem. In Jerusalem there is a holy mountain called the Temple Mount. During the time of King Solomon, the son of King David, a glorious Temple was built in order to worship Yahveh, ELOHIM, the God of the Universe. For many years, people from all over the nations would come to learn Torah and to inquire of Yahveh at that Temple. In the Temple there was an Outer Court where the Gentiles would come from all over the world to bring offerings to Yahveh, ELOHIM and to learn of His ways from His Levite priests that were officiating at that time. Even at that time, the promise that Yah gave to Abraham was coming to pass through the descendants of Abraham, the children of Israel. The families of the earth, the nations of the earth were being blessed as they came to worship Yah in Jerusalem and to inquire of His ways so that He might bless them. (For further study, see Genesis 15:5–7, Genesis 22:17–18, Genesis 26:4, Genesis 27:27–30, Numbers 22:12, Numbers 24:9, Exodus 32:13, Isaiah 2, Micah 4)

Israel is the only nation with which the God of the Universe has a covenant and until now it is still so. All of the blessings to the Gentiles come through the people of Israel, the original descendants of Abraham, Isaac, and Jacob, with whom the covenant was made. God's only covenant is with Abraham, his descendants, and all of those that:

- Join in with Israel
- Bless Israel

In other words God is not obligated to bless any nation unless that nation, joins in with Israel and blesses Israel. Those are the only stipulations for the blessing of the nations. Are they good to Israel or are they not? Are they walking in the ways of the God of Israel as given to Israel or are they not?

This is *the key* for the salvation and the blessing of the nations. This key has been lost for nearly 1,900 years, but now it is being restored. When it is fully restored, the salvation of the nations will follow, and only then we will offer to the Father many SHEEP NATIONS!

**I will bless those that bless you, and I will curse him who curses you and in you (Abram) all the families of the earth will be blessed.**

**Genesis 12:3**

Now let us study this verse from the Hebrew:

The word for "blessing" here is *bracha*. *Lebarech* from the word *bracha* means to "decree a word of life, goodness, favor, health, success and prosperity over someone that will be followed with many wonderful and positive events and opportunities that will bring great joy, happiness, wholeness, prosperity, greatness, abundance, fruitfulness and fulfillment"! (See Deuteronomy 28:1–14)

There are two words used in the Hebrew for the word curse, one of them is *klala* and the other one is *meera*.

*Klala* comes from the word *kal*, which means "light," as in not heavy. It means "those that take you lightly and do not honor or respect you as My chosen one." The same word is used for those that curse father or mother.

**And he that curses his father or his mother shall surely be put to death.**

**Exodus 21:17**

In other words those that disrespect their parents will die! Taking parents lightly, mocking them, *not listening to their instructions,* or disrespecting them brings evil occurrences to one's life.

*Meera* means "to issue a *word decree for the destruction of someone followed by all manner of evil occurrences* that will bring anguish, distress, grief, sickness, confusion, loss, lack, bankruptcy, loneliness, strife, rejection, futility, fear, failure, terror, self-destruction and total annihilation." (See Deuteronomy 28:14–68)

Notice that in both cases, both the blessing and the curse, *it is connected with issuing a decree or speaking a word*. From the beginning everything is created by ELOHIM issuing a decree and speaking His Word:

> In the beginning ELOHIM created the heavens and the earth. The earth was without form, and void; and darkness was on the face of the deep. And the Spirit of ELOHIM was hovering over the face of the waters. Then ELOHIM said: "Let there be light"; and there was light.
>
> Genesis 1:3

This is the golden rule: The only thing that is needed for something to be created is that ELOHIM would speak it. When He issues a curse, it is done by His Word; when He issues a blessing, it is done by His Word.

Look how Yeshua, by His Word, causes a fig tree to die:

And seeing a fig tree by the road, He came to it and found nothing on it but leaves, and said to it, "Let no fruit grow on you ever again." Immediately the fig tree withered.

Matthew 21:19

Now I will paraphrase Genesis 12:3.

"I will issue a decree and speak a word that will bring goodness, favor, wholeness, prosperity, peace, abundance, happiness, joy and fulfillment into those that speak good of you (Abraham and Israel) and do you good and cause you wholeness, prosperity, peace, abundance, happiness, joy and fulfillment. And I will issue a decree and speak a word of destruction, that will bring all manner of evil, sickness, disfavor, poverty, lack, failure, strife, anguish, rejection, grief, restlessness, futility, self-destruction and total annihilation to those that speak lightly of you, dishonor you, disrespect you, and don't listen to your instructions."

When people and nations take Israel lightly; disrespecting, mocking or even ignoring the descendants of Abraham, these people and these nations immediately enter into the road map of cursing. The only way out is through humility and repentance, otherwise they shall surely be visited with evil until they are annihilated.

The Key of Abraham can open nations to the blessing or lock nations out of the blessing and favor of Yah.

CHAPTER 6

# Choosing the Blessing or the Curse for Your Nation

*"For thus says the LORD of Hosts: 'He sent me after glory, to the nations which plunder you; for he who touches you touches the apple of His eye."*

— ZECHARIAH 2:8

There is no nation on the face of the earth that will be spared Yah's judgment IF they have 'touched,' harmed, or opposed His plans for Israel.

The following is an excerpt from the book, *Israel the Blessing or the Curse*, by John McTernan & Bill Koenig:

> The following organizations, which represent billions of people, have spoken out against Israel and God's covenant land and/or written President Bush and Secretary of State Colin Powell. They have all publicly

called for implementation of the Mitchell Plan from May 6, 2001 to August 31, 2001:

- The Vatican
- World Council of Churches
- The United Nations
- The European Union
- The Arab League
- China (McTernan, Koenig)

Look at what the Bible has to say about those that try to take the Land of Israel away from the people of Israel. The Almighty has restored Israel to its land after almost 2,000 years of exile. No other nation besides Israel has ever recovered from such a long exile and from so many attempts to destroy it. So whoever touches her makes God *very* upset.

**"For behold Your enemies make a tumult, and those who hate You have lifted up their head. They have taken crafty counsel against Your people, and consulted together against Your sheltered ones. They have said, 'Come, and let us cut them off from being a nation, that the name of Israel may be remembered no more...' So pursue them with Your tempest, frighten them with Your storm, fill their faces with shame, that they may seek Your name, O Lord."**

**Psalms 83:2-4,15**

Many nations are suffering right now and have suffered over the past few years since the beginning of the Peace Accords in Oslo. They've suffered from tempests, storms, and shame due to bankruptcy. Most of the nations of the world have sided with the Palestinian cause against Israel and have not risen to defend Israel from Palestinian terror.

As a result, Yah has plagued the land of many nations with terrible disasters such as the devastating current of El Niño in Ecuador, horrendous floods and hurricanes in the United States, earthquakes in Turkey, financial collapses all over Asia, Mexico and Argentina. And now the plague of SARS that is causing the loss of thousands of lives and millions of dollars due to the closing of the borders of many nations.

Commerce and tourism are collapsing in many nations now. Why? Because the Intifada, Arafat's campaign seeking to destroy Israel through terror, has caused the collapse of Israel's tourist industry. Many hotels have closed and thousands of people have become unemployed while the whole world stands watching, doing nothing to stop it. In fact, most nations have been speaking out against Israel justifying the 'Palestinian cause' without knowing that they have made themselves the enemies of Yahveh. They have touched the apple of His eye, and He is not keeping silent.

See the following quote *from Israel the Blessing or the Curse:*

> "President Clinton met with President Assad of Syria and boldly said that Israel had to give away the Golan Heights to Syria. Within twenty-four hours the land of America was rocked with the powerful Northridge earthquake. President Clinton met with Arafat and publicly rebuked Israel. Within twenty-four hours, Arkansas, the President's homeland, was hit by devastating tornados. Arafat then tours America, and during the exact time of

the tour, some of the worst flooding hits the land of the Ohio Valley...

In March and April 1997, the U.N. condemned Israel over Jerusalem, in July 1997, the U.N. called for a boycott of products coming from the land of Israel. In July 1997 an economic crisis started in Asia that touched the entire world. Billions of dollars were needed to try and stabilize these nations. Nations whose economies seemed to be endlessly growing were reduced to poverty!" (McTernan, Koenig)

**So pursue them with your tempest, frighten them with your storm, fill their faces with shame, that they may seek Your name, O LORD.**

Psalm 83:15

Were the nations frightened enough to seek the Name of the LORD? Hardly! On September 11, 2001, the World Trade Center in New York was hit by terrorism, shaking the world and its finances. For the first time, America felt what Israel has endured for so many years due to the constant terror attacks we have had to suffer. Interestingly enough, a Jewish architect has redesigned the World Trade Center being rebuilt in its original site. If America listens and repents from trying to force Israel into a road map, establishing a Palestinian state in the Land given to Abraham, she will be blessed beyond description. But if not... judgment will surely follow.

Yah's words to Abraham:

**And I will establish my covenant between Me and you and your seed after you in their generations for an everlasting**

covenant, to be a God unto you, and to your seed after you. And I will give unto you and to your seed after you the land where you are a stranger, all the land of Canaan for an everlasting possession, and I will be their God.

Genesis 17:7–8

In the year 2000, the Holy Spirit redirected me from a ministry trip to Costa Rica to travel to Washington DC. He said to me: "I want you to pray George W. Bush into the presidency of the United States. I want you to do this as an Israeli."

At that time it seemed impossible that George W. would win the elections. The whole election process was 'stuck' at the Supreme Court in Florida. Later on we realized that the difference in votes between Al Gore and Bush was the exact number of Jews that were refused entry to the United States in that exact county during the Second World War. These Jews were on board a ship called the St. Louis escaping Germany and the horrors of the Nazi Death Camps. When they sought shelter in the United States, President Roosevelt refused them entry. Eventually they were returned to Europe where most of them died in concentration camps. God did not forget that, and He was reminding America that the election of Bush was conditional...

**I will bless them that bless you and I will curse him who curses you.**

Genesis 12:3a

When I arrived in Washington DC, doors miraculously opened for me to tour the Congress and the Senate with an insider, the widow of a late congressman, who knew George W.

Bush very well. Because of her, we were allowed to pray in the Congressmen Chapel at Speaker's Corner. As we knelt to pray, the Holy One of Israel told me:

"Biblical politics. If Bush will exercise biblical politics over these two issues: The internal, moral affairs of the United States and biblical politics concerning Israel, I will bless him more than any other president before him. But if he doesn't..."

**For the day of the LORD upon all the nations, is near; as you have done it shall be done to you; your reprisal shall return upon your own head.**

**Obadiah 15**

China and Far Eastern nations have spoken against Israel and have not stood with her against her enemies. Now in the year 2003, they have been hit with the worst plague in a long time, the SARS. From an insider's information, someone that is connected with The World Bank in Hong Kong, I have received a message that SARS originated from pigs. Of course, they don't want anyone to know about this because the pig industry is very big in the Far East (and all over the world for that matter). Can you imagine if people were scared of eating pigs? Yes, I can imagine! They would be blessed, because the holy Torah and Eternal Laws of Yah say that pigs are unclean animals, and He has no shadow of turning in Him. (See Leviticus 11 for a thorough list of clean and unclean animals).

A year ago I was in Houston, preaching about the Jewish roots of the faith and the Dietary Laws. I said that the Dietary Laws are still for today as God's Laws are unchanging. He created some animals for food and sacrifice and some to be unclean, garbage disposers and carnivorous. I then explained how many people that eat pork suffer from epileptic-like seizures because of a worm from the pig that gets into their brains. As I was praying for people, a mother brought me her son in his thirties – he looked backwards, mentally oppressed, and distressed. "He has a worm in the brain," she said, "and takes medication." He had already stopped eating pork (ham, bacon and the like), yet *the worm remained*. That is the curse that happens when we violate the Torah instructions of the LORD in the name of 'freedom.'

I broke the curse in this man's life, and was happy to hear a few months later that he no longer had epileptic seizures and was bright, alert, and on fire for God!

In the same way, when the nations choose to adopt Yah's Laws and standards of righteousness and exercise biblical politics concerning Israel, they will enter into the blessing instead of the cursing of Abraham.

During the sixteenth century the Black Plague hit Europe and millions died. However, no one died among the Jews. The cause for that plague was also pigs. Later they masked it, and said that it came from the rats. Whether pigs or rats, both are unclean animals not to be eaten. The Jews kept the Dietary Commandments, so they suffered no plague. However, instead of learning the Torah from them, the nations blamed the Jews for causing the plague!

During December of 1996 and January and February of 1997, the Holy Spirit told me to go to Switzerland at the rate of once a month, in order to call people for a night watch and a whole Shabbat of prayer. During these three consecutive months, our assignment was to pray for Switzerland to release the Jewish gold that had been stolen by Nazi Germany from the Jews during the Holocaust and deposited in Swiss banks. Switzerland did not want to give that gold back to its rightful owners, so Yahveh sent me to pray and call Swiss people to repent for their nation's sin.

During the first prayer watch, I decreed prophetically: *"Because Switzerland has refused to give this gold back, the Swiss Franc is coming down!"* When I came back a month later the Swiss Franc had devaluated twenty percent and the Swiss people were shaking. At some point later, as an answer to our prayers, a portion of the church in Switzerland held a demonstration in Bern, the capital, in front of *Bundeshous*, the government house. Following this, within a few months, Switzerland released a certain percentage of that gold. But it's not yet over.

We came across a newspaper on board a flight to France during Passover in 2003 which detailed how many Jewish families were demanding the return of their wealth, what had been stolen by the anti-Semitic Vichy government during the Second World War. Altogether they demanded the restitution of millions of euros. If all the Jewish families that have been robbed by the nations resulting from persecution demanded their money back, they would empty all the world banks!

The Vatican holds a tremendous quantity of treasures stolen from the Jews during the times of the Spanish Inquisition that spanned nearly 400 years! In fact, it continued until the 19th Century. Many nations of Latin America such as Mexico, Peru, Chile and others, plundered much wealth from the Jews when the tribunals of the Inquisition moved over there.

The English, the French, the Russians, the Ukrainians and many others owe millions to the Jews that they dispossessed, persecuted, and threw out of their lands during pogroms and Jewish expulsions.

Many Polish citizens are living in stolen Jewish houses and property. This was also the plunder of the 3 million Jews of

Poland exterminated, with their cooperation, by the Nazis in their land. The same is true for many of the Hungarian citizens, and of course, the Germans.

The United States still owes money to a Jew that issued a loan to George Washington in order to bail America out of the war of independence against England. This Jew is commemorated on the dollar bill by a Star of David, but the loan was never repaid and that Jewish family is still owed that money.

Businesses all over Europe were stolen from the Jews during Second World War. All over the Arab nations, Jewish property has been plundered and stolen… and now the LORD has a controversy with the nations…

"A noise will come to the ends of the earth – For the LORD has a controversy with the nations; He will plead His case with all flesh. He will give those who are wicked to the sword,' says the LORD. Thus says the LORD, 'Behold disaster will go from nation to nation, and a great whirlwind shall be raised up from the farthest parts of the earth. And on that day the slain of the LORD shall be from one end of the earth, even to the other end of the earth. They shall not be lamented or buried; they shall become refuse on the ground."

Jeremiah 25:31–33

Just like the Jews have been refuse on the ground of many nations, Yah does not forget any nation that has plundered His people and He will be visiting one by one… He will also visit those that have not actively harmed, but have actively helped the Jews and Israel. They have stood by and watched. Those will be judged as goat nations:

For violence against your brother Jacob, shame shall cover you, and you shall be cut off forever – In that day that you stood on the other side, in the day that strangers carried captive his forces, when foreigners entered his gates and cast lots for Jerusalem – even you were as one of them...

> Obadiah 10–11

Deliver those who are drawn toward death, and hold back those stumbling to the slaughter. If you say, 'Surely we did not know this,' does not He who weighs the hearts consider it? He who keeps your soul, does He not know it? And will He not render to each man according to his deeds?

> Proverbs 24:11–12

Hear, you nations that sided with Hitler during Second World War, that have refused to give shelter to the Jews, or are siding with the Oslo Accords to carve up the land of Israel and serve portions of God's land to others. You nations that are standing on the fences, in 'neutrality,' you that have allowed terror to go unchecked and have not fought for Israel in the United Nations, this is what the Sovereign LORD says.

For the day of the LORD upon all nations is near; as you have done it shall be done to you; your reprisal shall return upon your own head.

> Obadiah 15

Has the Key of Abraham *locked* your nation from the blessing? This is how to *open* it, keep reading...

The Key of Abraham can open nations to the blessing or lock nations out of the blessing and favor of Yah.

CHAPTER 7

# Turn the Key of Abraham Into the Blessing Position

*And in you all the families of the earth will be blessed.*
— GENESIS 12:3B

By now I believe that you are getting a much better picture of the will of Yah concerning the nations. He really desires to bless all of them. He does not want one goat nation! That is why He chose Abraham. Yah wanted to redeem all of mankind from the curse of Adam. He wanted His creation back to Himself, and that is why He sent His only Son to walk the earth as a man and to suffer on that horrendous Roman cross in Jerusalem. It was so that the curse that all mankind deserved could be removed. That all of mankind could move into the blessing. However, Yeshua came as the fulfillment of the Abrahamic Covenant. He did not come to replace it, He came to keep the promise given by Yah to Abraham. That is why He had to be born a Jew – because the blessing to the nations is *only* through Abraham and His present day descendants, the Jewish people. So, the Messiah who would become the blessing to the nations had to be a Jew!

One of the most hideous, deceptive plans of satan has been to hide the fact that Yeshua, the Messiah, is Jewish. That is why when the Gentile portion of the church divorced from the Jews and the Torah in year AD 325 and set up an alternative system called 'Christianity,' it actually divorced itself from the blessing of Abraham. If Yeshua is Jesus Christ, a 'gentile god,' then the promise of Yahveh is a lie. Then there is no need for Abraham or the Jews. But, Yah never lies!

One way the enemy, through the Gentile portion of the church, has hidden the real identity of the Messiah as a Jew is by replacing days and seasons. Instead of celebrating the holy Days that He celebrated in obedience to the Torah of His Father, this anti- Messiah system has been celebrating pagan feasts instead! Yah is holy, and He would not have a mixture of paganism in His church! The real bride of Messiah, the ecclesia, has to shake herself off from this deceptive pagan system and STOP celebrating pagan deities in the guise of holy feasts.

Christmas day, the 25th of December, was borrowed from the pagans, as it was the day to celebrate the birth of their sun-god, Tammuz, to a virgin goddess called Semiramis. The Messiah was not born on the 25th of December. In fact that date is not a Hebrew biblical date as it belongs to the pagan Roman calendar. Yeshua was born according to the Hebrew biblical calendar. He was born during the Feast of Tabernacles, one of the three holy Feasts of pilgrimage to Jerusalem. It normally falls between September and October. It changes every year, as the Hebrew calendar is not ruled by the sun, but combines sun and moon together. (Zechariah 14:17–19, Leviticus 23)

One of the most prevalent practices of Christmas is the decoration of Christmas trees.

Thus says the LORD: "Do not learn the way of the gentiles; do not be dismayed at the signs of heaven, for the gentiles are dismayed at them. For the customs of the peoples are futile; for one cuts a tree from the forest, the work of the hands of the workman, with the ax. They decorate it with silver and gold; they fasten it with nails and hammers so that it will not topple."

Jeremiah 10:2–4

Not only has the church learned the ways of the gentiles/pagans, but has been leading the nations into these pagan celebrations and pagan practices!

How many 'Christian' houses are filled with Christmas decorations for next year's celebration? This brings a curse to your own homes, and if believers of Messiah are not blessed, how can they bring the blessing to the nations? We are supposed to teach the nations holiness:

**Pursue peace with all people, and holiness without which no one will see the LORD.**

Hebrews 12:4

Pursuing peace without holiness is perversion. Yah instructs us to pursue peace *without compromising holiness*. One of the marks of grace in the nations is when there is an outpouring of the Holy Spirit and old men dream dreams, young men see visions and men and women prophesy (Joel 2, Acts 2). However, when there is no holiness in the church, there is no open vision and revelation, and the people perish.

The church (Jew and Gentile as *one*) is the carrier of the blessing of Abraham into the nations, but if the church is following pagan practices, she *shuts down the revelation of Messiah to the nations.* That is why in 2 Chronicles 7:14 it says:

"If My people that are called by My name humble themselves and pray and turn from their wicked ways, then I will hear from heaven and I will heal their land."

2 Chronicles 7:14

The LORD has been patiently waiting for His people to turn from pagan practices, pagan feasts, immorality, anti-Semitism and every unbiblical wicked way so He can heal the lands of the nations. It begins with you, your family and your church, as the obedience of one person can turn a nation around. He called us to be a royal priesthood, a holy nation!

So I sought for a man (as in mankind) among them who would make a wall, and stand in the gap before me on behalf of the land, that I should not destroy it; but I found not one. Therefore I have poured out My indignation on them; I have consumed them with the fire of My wrath; and I have recompensed their deeds on their own heads,' says Yahveh, ELOHIM.

Ezekiel 22:30–31

This is the strategy that Yahveh uses for the salvation of nations. He is always looking for a holy man or woman or group of priests that are willing to cleanse themselves from the pagan practices of the nations and come to obey His holy Laws and Commandments. This is how He began with Abraham, the one that would become the carrier of the blessing! He told him to leave his land, his family, and his pagan practices and to follow the LORD into an unknown land to worship Him alone.

Today the LORD is calling the Christians to get rid of pagan Christianity and all of the pagan feasts, ungodly practices, watered- down gospels, and ungodly men-pleasing attitudes, and to go back to the same Torah that Yeshua and His Jewish apostles, including Paul honored. He is calling the true church to arise as a royal priesthood and a holy nation, a people in whose heart is His Law, His Torah!

**Listen to me, you who know righteousness, you people in whose heart is my Law; do not fear the reproach of men, nor be afraid of their insults. For the moth will eat them up as a garment, and the worm will eat them like wool; but My righteousness will be forever, and My salvation from generation to generation.**

Isaiah 51:7–8

Listen to me you saints of Yah who desire to follow the LORD's Commandments and abandon all pagan feasts and return to the holy Feasts of the LORD. Listen to me all of you holy people that desire to stop eating pork, shrimp, and unclean, profane animals that cause worms in the brain and in the body. Listen to me those that desire to honor Shabbat in your lives as the fourth Commandment in Deuteronomy 5 commands (not suggests!). Listen to me and do not let the mockery and pressure of your 'brothers and sisters' stop you from obeying Yah, for He is calling a holy people unto Himself *without which the nations will not be saved!*

The fear of man is a snare, and Yah has called us to fear Him and Him alone. Be careful of those preachers that try to pressure you using the writings of Paul the Apostle. These writings have been misinterpreted for nearly 1800 years and have been used to persecute and kill the Jews. Paul's words have been distorted to invent doctrines that have caused the annihilation of many millions of Jews. Do not even argue with them, but rather pray that the LORD removes the blindness from their eyes. This blindness has been in the church for over 18 centuries!

Gentile theologians, with no understanding of Pharisaic traditions, customs, and idioms, have endeavored to interpret Rabbi Paul's writings spanning the last 16 centuries. Even Peter, a Jew, had a problem with interpreting Paul! These men have exalted the words of Paul above the words of the Master Yeshua Himself, which are so clear:

**Do not think that I came to destroy the Law or the prophets, I did not come to destroy but to fulfill. For assuredly I say to you, till heaven and earth pass away, one jot or one title will by no means pass from the Law until all is fulfilled. Whoever therefore breaks the least of these Commandments, and teaches men so, shall be called least in the kingdom of heaven; but whoever does and teaches them, he shall be called great in the kingdom of heaven. For I say to you, that unless your righteousness exceeds the righteousness of the Pharisees, you will by no means enter the kingdom of heaven.**

Matthew 5:17–20

It was Paul who said:

And it came to pass after three days that Paul called the leaders of the Jews together. So when they had come together, he said to them: "Men and brethren, though I have done nothing against our people or the customs of our fathers, yet I was delivered as a prisoner from Jerusalem into the hands of the Romans."

Acts 28:17

Was Paul lying to them? He said that he kept even the customs, not to mention the Torah!

For I delight in the Law of God according to the inward man. But I see another law in my members, warring against the law of my mind, and bringing me into captivity to the law of sin which is in my members. O wretched man that I am! Who will deliver me from this body of death? I thank God, through Yeshua The Messiah our LORD! So then with the mind I myself serve the Law of God, but with the flesh the law of sin. There is therefore now no condemnation to those who are in Messiah Yeshua who do not walk according to the flesh but according to the Spirit. For the Law of the Spirit of life in the Messiah Yeshua has made me free from the law of sin and death.

Romans 7:22–8:2

All of Paul's writings must be in line with the teachings of Yeshua. Yeshua was a Torah observant Jewish Rabbi. He celebrated no pagan feasts, neither did He command us to do so. He paid the price on the cross so that we can get free from the law of sin and death not from the Law of God! Adam caused all of mankind to fall into the curse because he disobeyed

Elohim's only law, which was, by the way, a 'Dietary law' – *"Do not eat of the tree of knowledge of good and evil."* Yeshua paid the price for Adam's disobedience and all of our disobedience, so that we could become obedient like Him. The power of the true gospel is not that we are 'free from the Law of Yah,' but that we are free from *the law of sin and death.*

Most of the church that is 'free from the Law of God' is now 'captive to the law of sin and death.'

"The Torah written in the minds and hearts by the Holy Spirit" (Jeremiah 31:31-34) is the true mark of the New Covenant, which is actually the Renewed Covenant from Abraham until Yeshua and was given to Israel. The Holy Spirit becomes our Torah teacher! He would never lead us to celebrate pagan feasts, break any of the Commandments including the Shabbat, lay with our husbands at the time of our period, lie, manipulate, or fornicate. Neither will He lead us to eat unclean animals such as pork, or to eat or drink blood. We are called to be holy people, led by the Holy Spirit of Yah, who will only lead us to obey Yahveh's Commandments.

I love the story of the mighty apostle of faith, Smith Wigglesworth, whose wife taught him how to read using the Bible alone. Smith never read any 'Christian writings or theological debates!' He read only the Bible. When asked to say the blessing at a banquet serving roasted pig, he prayed:

> "Dear Father if you can bless what you have cursed, then bless this pig."

He knew the Torah because the Holy Spirit had written it in his heart because he read only the Scriptures and no other literature. Smith was so full of faith, power, and holiness that he did many creative miracles. He raised many people from the dead including his own wife!

Stop following erroneous Christian theology and let the Holy Spirit teach you the Scriptures. You too will become powerful and full of the glory of Yah!

We cannot obey Yah's Commandments except through the revelation and the empowerment of the Holy Spirit. Your own efforts will be futile. You cannot walk in righteousness and holiness unless you have an intimate and personal relationship with the Living God of Israel through Yeshua, the Messiah. He paid His price so that you would be filled with His Spirit, His Ruach, who will teach you His ways!

Any writing of Paul, where he seemed to be opposing God's Laws, feasts, or holy days has been seriously misinterpreted. He was not opposing the Law. He was opposing the religious spirit of the Galatians that were trying to get saved by the Law rather than by the blood of the Messiah. They were trying to be 'holy' by self-effort rather than by faith and by submission to the Spirit of Truth within them. He was coming against *legalism* not the Law. Legalism is a prideful, erroneous attitude of the heart of which needs to be repented. We can do nothing apart from the revelation and empowerment of the Holy Spirit.

> "Therefore the Law is holy, and the Commandment holy, just and good,"
>
> Romans 7:12

Maybe this is a good time to pray! Are you legalistic or are you Lawless? Both of them are unclean, so please pray with me this short revolutionary prayer:

*"Dear Father in heaven, thank you for the blood atonement of your Son Yeshua, my Jewish Messiah. I receive full forgiveness through this blood atonement, and I receive Yeshua, the Jewish Messiah, of the seed of Abraham into my heart. I renounce all forms of legalism and Lawlessness, including the celebration of pagan feasts. I ask you to fill me with your Holy Spirit and write your Torah in my heart. Please teach me your ways and teach me to obey your Commandments. Use me to love Israel in action and to bring the blessing of Abraham to the nations. In Yeshua's name, I pray. Amen!"*

Yeshua sent His Jewish disciples to make disciples of all nations and to teach His Commandments to the nations. His Commandments and His Father's Commandments are the same. He said, "I and the Father are *one*" (John 10:30).

When we keep the Commandments and we teach them, we become great. Only great people can bring the blessing of Abraham to the nations. It takes great people to bring great nations before the Throne of the Great King. The church has been filled with little people that break the Laws of Yah, because of deep ignorance and rebellion. Yeshua said that those that break the *least of these Commandments, they shall be called least in the kingdom.*

It takes great people to bring nations to the kingdom. I am inviting you to become great by obeying Yah's Commandments and teaching the nations to do so...

**Now it shall come to pass, if you diligently obey the voice of Yahveh your Elohim, to observe carefully all His**

Commandments which I command you today, that the LORD your God will set you high above all the nations of the earth.

> Deuteronomy 28:1

Any nation that will set the Torah of Yahveh as their righteous Constitutional Standard will be set on high and will become great.

In Exodus 12 we see that a mixed multitude from the nations escaped Egypt with Israel and also received the Torah together with Israel. That is why the first Gentile followers of Yeshua the Messiah were God-fearing and following Torah. Though they had not converted to Judaism, they honored Yah's righteous Laws and standards and studied Torah with the Jews.

We were in France a few weeks ago with a dear friend and powerful revivalist. He had been studying Torah with us and was teaching his followers to love Israel and Yah's holy standards. He invited us to teach them and their followers about the biblical Feast of Passover. Typically, when we carry this message, the LORD confirms it with signs, wonders and miracles. Because this message carries the blessing of Abraham to the nations, curses are broken, people are made whole in spirit, soul and body, revival comes to their lives, and there is a fresh outpouring of prophetic revelation into them… By the grace of Yah, we carry an anointing from the Father to break curses and take individuals, families, churches and nations to the blessing of Abraham as we preach the truth that sets them FREE!

But what impressed me the most during this time of ministry in France was the following:

Our revivalist friend and his beautiful wife went for a walk in the Champs Elysees between meetings. While walking, a lady approached them and offering them chocolate 'Easter bunnies.'

Our friends knew by then that Easter is a pagan celebration that exalts a Babylonian deity, the goddess Ishtar. That the bunny rabbits represent Babylonian fertility-based orgies.

Every year the Babylonians, and later the Romans, would celebrate Easter, Ishtar, through orgies. A year later, the 3-month old babies born of these orgies were sacrificed to Ishtar, in order to bring fertility and prosperity. They would dip eggs into the blood of these sacrificed babies and proceed to hang the eggs as 'decorations.' Each 'blood painted' egg represented one sacrificed baby. That is where the tradition of the painted Easter eggs is coming from! The rabbits are the Babylonian symbol of fertility. So, during Easter, they sell chocolate bunnies, chocolate eggs, painted bunnies and painted eggs.

Our revivalist friend proceeded to firmly explain to this woman the real meaning of Easter and of the eggs and the bunnies. She was so convicted and disgusted from this explanation that *she immediately stopped selling them.*

Our friend did exactly what Yeshua said in Matthew 28:19: *"Make disciples of all nations, teaching them to obey all that I have commanded you."* This couple in France has the greatness that it takes to bring SHEEP NATIONS before the Throne of the Father. By walking and teaching Torah, they have set themselves apart for greatness. For personally enjoying and carrying the blessing of Abraham to the nations. This kind of spirit is what it takes to stop plagues such as SARS and others! This kind of spirit is what it takes in order to stop the financial plague that has been hitting the world.

They do not only teach Torah to France, but they are actively involved in blessing Israel through support and tourism at a time that others are afraid to come to the Land because of terror. I also know that they have a plan to help many Jews make

Aliyah and return to their own land. Through them the blessing of Abraham is reaching France, who has been one of the most anti-Semitic nations. Holy priests who walk in righteousness can turn even very wicked nations around. Yahveh has found someone to stand in the gap for France, and we will hear much more about this in the days to come. What about you and your nation? He is looking for KEY people like this in every nation. He is no respecter of persons. He will make you great if you obey Him:

**For the eyes of the LORD run to and fro throughout the whole earth, to show himself strong on behalf of those whose heart is loyal to Him.**

**2 Chronicles 16:9**

CHAPTER 8

# The Blessing of Abraham – Full Wages!

*And in you all the families of the earth will be blessed.*
— GENESIS 12:3B

I am going to teach you how to defeat the financial plague hitting many nations. Whether you are a businessman, businesswoman, a preacher, or you are on a salary or pension, this chapter is for you!

Dear friend, a real child of Abraham cannot be part of the financial problem of the earth. He has to be part of the solution! We are destined to bring nations to become SHEEP NATIONS, blessed nations. John 10:10 tell us who the thief is:

**The thief does not come except to steal, kill and to destroy. I have come that they may have life, and that they may have it more abundantly.**

John 10:10

Both financial plagues and health plagues are the opposite of life. They are pure death, and they bring anguish, distress and unhappiness. Our God is a good God! He sent His Son to the earth to bring life, life eternal, and life in abundance. That has always been His desire for man.

> The LORD God planted a garden eastward in Eden, and there He put the man that He had formed. And out of the ground the LORD God made every tree grow that is pleasant to the sight and good for food, the tree of life was also in the midst of the garden and the tree of knowledge of good and evil.
>
> **Genesis 2:8–9**

From the beginning, ELOHIM desired man and woman to live in abundance in a pleasant atmosphere, surrounded by life, beauty and provision. Had the woman and the man not harbored lust and doubt in their hearts so as to listen to the snake, we would still be in that Garden today! But Yeshua came to restore us to that place that we lost. He took upon Himself the entirety of the curse that we deserve because of sin and disobedience. He became poor that we may become rich (2 Corinthians 8:9). He took stripes upon Himself that we might be healed. He carried all of our grief and sorrows (Isaiah 53). There is absolutely no better news than this. He came to heal the broken hearted, to make whole those that are bruised, to make free those that are in captivity and in any type of bondage, to remove our mourning and pain and to cover us with joy and praise (Isaiah 61). There is just simply no better news than this! He came to give us life, abundant life. The life that we lost due to sin and disobedience.

As we put our trust in Him and begin the road of obedience, He restores our souls, bodies, finances, and families. Sometimes the devastation of our life has been so great that the process of restoration takes time. We receive immediately a new spirit, a new heart, in order to commune with Yah, but our minds need retraining. We need to learn the way of faith and obedience which is foreign to us. We have to learn the way of love and forgiveness and rid ourselves of the fear, anxiety and shame that has plagued our lives. We have to learn how to walk in the blessing, as our minds have only known the curse!

During all financial crises in history, the Jews have been persecuted, blamed and made the scapegoat, and the church has never arisen to defend them from the onslaught and to teach the nations to bless them! Because of this, there have been many national devastations. The more the nations turn against the Jews, the more they suffer, and this is what Satan wants!

This time as the world has been hit by a financial plague, it's time for the church to teach the nations the Key of Abraham. The only solution for this financial plague to stop is:

Repent from trying to manipulate Israel out of her inheritance by exchanging land for peace. Begin to actively bless and support her as she builds settlements for the new immigrants that are coming, and will be coming, from all over the world. This will turn the finances of nations around quickly!

The same will work with you as an individual in the church. Begin to pray and give into the Messianic body in Israel, and you will see a turnaround if you do it in faith, love and obedience. The following is my paraphrase from the Hebrew on Psalms 122:6.

**Pray and inquire for the well-being, peace and prosperity of Jerusalem, Israel and the Jewish people. As you pray for her**

and actively and practically see to it that Jerusalem is blessed, you will be blessed, made whole and prosperous as well.

Psalms 122:6

The following is my paraphrase on Psalms 137:5–6

If I forget you O Jerusalem, Israel and Jewish people, let my right hand forget its cunning, its ability to work, write, play instruments, cook, caress and provide. Let my tongue stick to my palate, so I cannot speak, preach, prophesy or sing, if I do not consider Jerusalem, Israel and the Jewish people as my greatest joy and love.

Psalms 137:5–6

Now I give you the *Key*: Yah chose Abraham because He knew he would embrace His Commandments and teach his children after him.

Since Abraham shall surely become a great and mighty nation, and all the nations of the earth shall be blessed in him. For I have known him, in order that he may command his children and his household after him, that they keep the way of the LORD, to do righteousness and justice, that the LORD may bring to Abraham what He had spoken to him.

Genesis 18:18–19

This is what Yah says to Isaac, Abraham's chosen son:

And I will make your descendants multiply as the stars of heaven; I will give your descendants all these lands; and in your seed all the nations of the earth shall be blessed. Because Abraham obeyed my voice and kept my charge, my Commandments, my statutes and my Laws.

**Genesis 26:4,5**

Anyone in the world who chooses to follow the way of Abraham will be blessed. Abraham left his culture and his fathers idols. He left his land and joined himself to the Lord Yahveh to obey Him and do His will.

Any person or any nation that chooses to:
- Follow the way of Abraham
- Bless Israel and the Jews, the descendants of Abraham

Any nation like that will be blessed, made whole and prosperous. Any family, any church, any individual. That is the principle of the blessing of Abraham.

## The Story of Ruth

There is one woman in the Bible that did that and managed to get herself out from under an eternal curse that was upon her people and into the blessing of Abraham. She did exactly what is written here. She left her own pagan, idol-worshipping culture, she joined in with Israel and with Israel's God and Torah. She blessed Israel, and she became one of the most prominent women in the Bible. She had nothing going for her. Her only future was to be under a curse forever, but she chose the way of Abraham. She left the curse and entered into the blessing of Abraham. That woman is none other than Ruth the Moabitess.

Yah is calling for *Ruth nations*, because *Ruth nations* become Sheep Nations. They enter into the full blessing of Abraham and receive *full wages* and *full rewards*.

Let us learn about Ruth. Her background story is quite tragic. She was married to the son of Naomi, a Jewish woman from Bethlehem. Naomi was not living in Judea anymore. Because of a drought, she had moved to the enemy country of Moab with her husband hoping to find prosperity. This couple was running from their inheritance in the Land of Israel and was looking for prosperity in a land that was cursed. So, of course, they found no prosperity, but rather tragedy, death and poverty. Naomi's husband Elimelech and her two sons died in a plague. (Maybe they had left the ways of Torah, and they had been eating some pork or other unclean animals.) One of the sons that died was the husband of Ruth, as both the sons had married pagan women.

Resulting from this tragedy, Naomi, the mother-in-law, awakens to the fact that she is in a foreign and Lawless land and that Yah has not blessed her there. So, she decides to return (which is another word for repent) to her inheritance in Bethlehem, Judea, in the Land of Israel.

As she bid her two daughters-in-law farewell, one of them kissed her and departed to go back to her family and her gods, yet Ruth chose to stick with her and go all the way to Israel with her.

These are the eternal words that Ruth said to Naomi, this Jewish widow. These words resonate through the ages. They changed the course and the destiny of Ruth and of the nation of Israel forever:

**But Ruth said, "entreat me not to leave you, or to turn back from following after you for wherever you will go, I will go; And wherever you lodge, I will lodge, your people shall be my people, and your God my God. Where you die, I will die, and**

there I will be buried. The LORD do so to me, and more also, if anything but death parts you and me."

Ruth 1:16–17

Please understand that Ruth was a Moabitess and the Moabites could not stay with the Jewish people. In fact there was no way that a Moabite could join with and become part of the Jewish nation, since they were under a curse for not helping the Israelites at the time of their need in the desert:

**An Ammonite or Moabite shall not enter the assembly of the LORD; even to the tenth generation none of his descendants shall enter the assembly of the LORD forever. Because they did not meet you with bread and water on the road when you came out of Egypt, and because they hired against you Balaam the son of Beor from Pethor of Mesopotamia to curse you.**

Deuteronomy 23:3–4

None of the descendants of the Moabites, including Ruth, could ever come into the assembly of the LORD, which are the people of Israel. So when Ruth was joining herself with this Jewish woman, with her people and her God and His Commandments, she was taking a great risk. Would they accept her? Would she be rejected by them and be left destitute from both sides, no Moab and no Israel? Maybe they would even kill her. But her faith and love were stronger than her fear. She loved that Jewish woman, and she had received a revelation from Yahveh. The same one that you can receive today as you read the pages of this book: That if she joined herself to love and to bless this Jewish woman and her people Israel; if she chose her Living God and His Torah, she could come out from under the curse and get into the blessing. Without fully knowing, she was turning the Key of Abraham into the blessing position!

**I will bless those that bless you… and in you (Abraham, your God, your people) all the families of the earth (including the cursed Moabites) will be blessed.**

**Genesis 12:3 (paraphrased)**

The blessing is always stronger than the curse. Even so today, as all nations are under a curse, if they follow the way of Abraham, the way of Ruth, their curses will break, and the blessing will come flooding in.

Later on we see Ruth, gleaning barley as a poor widow, in the fields of one of the major princes of the town. He was a relative of Naomi. The Torah instructs us to always leave some food in the fields while harvesting, so that the poor, the orphan and the widow may eat. Naomi and Ruth were both poor and widows. They were far from looking blessed, but the blessing had been set in motion by Naomi's repentance and Ruth's momentous choice of blessing a Jew in her distress and joining in with her people and her God.

The moment that you do this, the blessing of Abraham is set in motion, even though it looks otherwise. Someone is watching your moves, actions and decisions… a full reward is on its way.

Boaz, the owner of the field, noticed Ruth as she was gleaning. She must have been dressed very humbly and in dark widow's garments, but somehow her face shone with the inner beauty of the obedient and the faithful. Did Boaz fall in love with her at first sight? I do not know, but I do know that he noticed her and seemed to have heard good things about her.

**Then Boaz said to Ruth, "You will listen my daughter, will you not? Do not glean in any other field, nor go from here, but stay close by my young women. Let your eyes be on the field which they reap, and go after them. Have I not commanded the young men not to touch you? And when you are thirsty, go to the vessels and drink from what the young men have drawn."**

Ruth 2:8-9

Now, this was pretty good. The sign of the blessing of Abraham had manifested itself, and that sign is *favo*r. Ruth had found favor with one of the major leaders and estate owners in town. She could have been rejected and mistreated because she was from Moab. After all, the Moabites deserved it. But she took the risk to love a Jew unconditionally, be faithful to her in her time of need (the opposite of her Moabite ancestors), and to join with her God, to walk in His ways. The outcome of that is always *favor*. Yahveh smiles at those people that choose the 'Ruth way'! "I will bless those who bless you, I will be favorable to them."

I have seen this happening many times in our own lives and ministries. There is literally no person that has ever worked with us and been faithful that has not received special favor from the LORD. Every time they have received what they needed and desired, but just like Ephesians 3:19 says, "Exceedingly, abundantly above all that we ask or think." I've seen some of our helpers go from bankruptcy to prosperity, from unemployment to full employment, from barrenness to fruitfulness, and from confusion to wholeness. The favor of Yah is always on those that are faithful to assist and to bless the Jewish people.

Ruth received favor from Boaz, but favor is only the sign of the blessing, and favor is always followed with a manifestation of the blessing!

**So she fell on her face, bowed down to the ground, and said to him, "Why have I found favor in your eyes, that you should take notice of me, since I am a foreigner?" And Boaz answered and said to her, "It has been fully reported to me, all that you have done for your mother-in-law since the death of your husband, and how you have left your father and your mother and the land of your birth, and have come to a people whom you did not know before."**

Ruth 2:10–11

In other words, "I have received all the information that I need about you. You are a lover of the Jews. You are faithful. You are courageous. You are willing to lose everything and risk everything in order to follow the God of Israel and bless His people."

So, here comes the blessing. Do you remember the definition of 'blessing'? "To speak a good word or a decree that will be followed with favorable and positive occurrences that will bring wholeness, prosperity and good things into one's life." A blessing begins with a spoken word. So Boaz said:

**The LORD repay your work, and a full reward be given you by the LORD God of Israel, under whose wings you have come for refuge.**

Ruth 2:12

My dear friends, nothing else can give you a better reward than this. The Ruth way is the Abraham way.

**I will bless those that bless you, curse him who curses you and in you all the families of the earth will be blessed.**

**Genesis 12:3**

The full blessing, the full wages, and the full reward of Ruth is still being collected to this day. That is the nature of a full reward from Yahveh, Elohim, the God of Israel. The reward is limitless. It never ends. Ruth, a forever cursed Moabite, a widow and a poor beggar, became the wife of the prince of Bethlehem, Boaz, and thus became a princess herself. She became the richest and most influential woman in town. Together they had a son that brought great restoration to old Naomi. This son, Obed, became the great grandfather of King David, of whose line was born Yeshua the Messiah. She is in the royal line of King David and of the Messiah Himself. There can be no greater honor than that! So Ruth's reward and her wages continue to be collected every time that one person receives forgiveness of sins through the sacrifice of Yeshua. Every time a person is born again. She is still collecting her wages in heaven, as she sits in the Cloud of Witnesses!

## A Time to Ponder

Think about your life. Think about your family and about your nation. Think about your business, your job, your health, your mental and emotional health and your children. Do you see the mark of the blessing? Maybe you see the marks of many curses. Maybe you, your family, and your church have been like the

Moabites. You have not cared for the descendants of Abraham, the Jewish people, and the nation of Israel. Maybe you belong to a nation that has done much harm to the Jews. Certainly, all have to one degree or another. But, I can promise you that as you follow the Ruth way and turn the Key of Abraham into the blessing position, your life will begin to shift. As you accept Yeshua the Jewish Messiah into your life and allow Yah's Torah and Commandments to be written in your heart, in due season all financial plagues and other plagues will leave. And you will show the marks of the blessing of Abraham and will be able to lead your family, your church, and even your ethnic group, your nation, into the blessing of Abraham. Begin today to turn your nation, ethnic group, language group or tribe into a *Sheep Nation* by making the choice that Ruth made as she followed Naomi.

Please pray with me:

> *"Dear heavenly Father, thank you for giving me the Key of Abraham and showing me the Ruth Way, out of the curse and into the blessing. I say just like Ruth: The God of Israel is my God, His Torah is my Torah and His people Israel are my people. I will stick with them and bless them as long as I live. Thank you for showing me ways to connect with them and bless them and for writing your Torah in my heart. I renounce all anti-Semitism, Christian theologies, and other ideologies that have taught me to hate the Jews and to hate your Torah, & I commit my life to you in a fresh new way. Fill me with your Holy Spirit that I might walk in your might and strength and in obedience to your Commandments. Teach me your ways and make me successful and prosperous as I demonstrate the blessing of*

*Abraham in my own life. Now, help me lead my nation into becoming a Sheep Nation. In Yeshua's name, Amen."*

My prayer for you

*"Father, I break any curse that has befallen my brother/sister because of sins of omission and / or sins of commission against the Jewish people and the nation of Israel. Let the curse be broken off of him/her and their children and their immediate family, even to the fourth or fifth generation. And now by the authority bestowed upon me, I bless him/her with the blessing of Abraham and with the full wages of Ruth, and I pray that you will help them to walk in your ways and be obedient to bless the Jews in practical ways. May he/she never compromise your truth, and may he/she live in your blessing all of their lives. Use him/her to lead his/her nation into becoming a Sheep Nation. I release favor and abundant life into him/her in Yeshua's name. Amen."*

And now I invite you to arise and decree this ancient prophetic blessing over Israel and these apostolic Jews that Yahveh is raising up in these End times to turn the nations back to Him.

**Arise and shine for your light has come! And the glory of Yahveh is risen upon you. For behold the darkness shall cover the earth, and deep darkness the people; but Yahveh will arise over you, and His glory will be seen upon you. The gentiles shall come to your light, and kings to the brightness of your rising. Lift up your eyes all around and see; they all gather together they come to you, your sons will come from afar and your daughters shall be nursed at your side. Then you shall see and become radiant, and your heart shall swell with joy, because the abundance of the sea shall be turned to you, the**

wealth of the gentiles shall come to you. Violence shall no longer be heard in your land, neither wasting nor destruction within your borders; but you shall call your walls salvation and your gates praise. Your sun shall no longer go down, nor shall your moon withdraw itself; for the LORD, Yahveh will be your everlasting light, and the days of your mourning shall be ended. Also your people shall all be righteous; they shall inherit the land forever, the branch of my planting, the works of my hands, that I may be glorified. A little one shall become a thousand, and a small one a strong nation. I, the LORD, Yahveh will hasten it in its time.

Isaiah 60

This is the time, the *moed*, the *kairos* moment, the divine opportunity for the church to arise and to return to its original holy foundations with Israel, the Jewish people and the Torah. This is the time for the church to turn from being a *Moabite* to a *Ruth*. From being one who throughout history has persecuted the Jews, including the Messianic Jews, into one who will stick to us, bless us, and together with us... Inherit the nations and bring forth the true Jewish Messiah, bringing Him to this very needy world. It took Boaz, a Jew, and Ruth, a Moabite, to bring forth the Messianic line. So it will take the Jews and the *Ruth-like Gentiles,* together, to birth this glorious restoration, redemption and transformation of nations into SHEEP NATIONS.

Notice that it was not Boaz that joined Ruth in Moab and its customs, but rather Ruth that joined in with Naomi, her God and her people. So it is with you, dear brothers and sisters among the Gentiles.

It is not we, the Jews, that need to join Christianity and its customs and traditions. We have been persecuted, hunted, and butchered since the time of Constantine, in attempt to escape the forceful conversions to Christianity. The Messianic Jews of that time could not agree to its tenets and pagan foundations, and neither can we agree now. Even though we have a lot to learn from one another in many areas, it is not the Jewish people that get grafted into Christianity, but rather it is the gentile believers that get grafted into Israel, Israel's God and Messiah, and Israel's Torah. As that order gets restored, the nations will come to us, and their kings to the brightness of our rising.

**And you being a wild olive tree, were grafted in among them, and with them became a partaker of the root and fatness of the olive tree.**

**Romans 11:17b**

I will bless those who bless you, and I will curse him who curses you; and in you all the families of the earth shall be blessed.

**Genesis 12:3**

CHAPTER 9

# The Master's Key For Greatness

*"Do not think that I came to destroy the Law or the Prophets, I did not come to destroy but to fulfill. For assuredly I say to you, till heaven and earth pass away, one jot, one title will by no means pass from the Law till all is fulfilled. Whoever therefore breaks the least of these Commandments, shall be called least in the kingdom of heaven; but whoever does and teaches them, he shall be called great in the kingdom of heaven,"*

— MATTHEW 5:17-19

The 120 disciples that were in the Upper Room of The Temple (Temple Mount of today) were following the Master's key for greatness. They were obeying the Commandment in the Torah about celebrating the Feast of Shavuot (Pentecost) in Jerusalem. Also, as is customary in those types of gatherings, they were praying and studying Torah together. They were both *doing the*

*Commandment* and *teaching it*. Greatness simply followed. The Holy Spirit fell like tongues of fire and sat on each one of them. When the Holy Spirit fell with such might, it did not fall on ignorant, disobedient pagans. It fell on Jewish disciples of Yeshua that had studied Torah with Him. He was their Rabbi for three and a half years, and now they were following His instructions.

Please notice that every time there is an outpouring of the Holy Spirit that impacts many, it is connected with these two factors:
- People are waiting on the LORD in prayer
- Torah is taught; holiness and obedience is taught

To the first outpouring you need to add another factor; they were celebrating a divine appointment with Yah, through the feasts. All of His feasts, as depicted in Leviticus 23 and throughout the Word, are divine dates or divine appointments with the Father.

Any group that sets themselves to seek Yah through prayer and to teach His Torah, His holy and righteous standards for living, plus keep the divine appointments of the feasts, is using the Master's key for greatness. Greatness surely follows. He will beautify those that seek Him in truth with His presence!

It is high time to stop being the least in the kingdom and become great!

As this apostolic move of the restoration of the Torah goes on, we will see more and more great disciples and great apostles arise. Yah has destined us for greatness, but rebellion and ignorance of His Torah, His divine appointments and holy standards has kept most of the church in a condition of 'smallness,' rather than *greatness*. It is not surprising that the nations of the world are not afraid of the ecclesia and that they keep on 'doing their own thing' without taking us into consideration. But it is *time* to shake off the Nicene Creed, and every deceptive 'church theology' that will keep us small. Yah is calling us to *greatness*.

Had the church been *great* at the time of the Second World War, it would have arisen as an Esther, and it would have stopped the Holocaust. The church has the authority to bind and to loose, which means "to forbid or to permit." It takes *great* people to have the boldness and courage to forbid wickedness. Yah is calling us to *greatness*.

The missing factor in the body is the *Torah*. As Yeshua says, he that does it and teaches it shall be great in the kingdom. No one can hate the Jews when they love the Torah. In fact anti-Semitism is totally connected with rejecting the Law, the eternal Word of Yah. A person that loves the Torah can never hate the people through which it came. Never!

It is the Torah that made the people of Israel great, and it is the Torah that will make you *great* today! Yeshua came to teach us how to walk it, not to abolish it. How could He abolish the Law of His Father? No, He came to give us a *full* interpretation, and then He sent the Holy Spirit, the Ruach HaKodesh, to continue the work. Satan has tried to diminish ELOHIM's Torah from the beginning. In the Garden He gave a Torah Instruction to Adam:

**And the LORD ELOHIM commanded the man saying, "Of every tree of the garden you may freely eat; but of the tree of knowledge of good and evil you shall not eat, for in the day that you eat of is you shall surely die."**

**Genesis 2:16–17**

Later on Satan, in the snake, came to the woman saying:

> Has ELOHIM indeed said, "You shall not eat of every tree of the garden?"
>
> **Genesis 3:1**

And then he proceeded to undermine Yah's Torah instruction by saying that there would be no consequences if she broke it. "You shall not surely die." In other words he was saying what many noted preachers say today: "The Law is not for today and if you break it you will suffer no consequences. You shall not surely die. You are free from the Law."

It is amazing how these preachers forget the warning of Acts 5 when a couple by the name of Ananias and Sapphira fell dead at the feet of Shimon Peter the apostle because they *lied* about their finances.

Since the apostles and all the believers lived a Torah observant lifestyle, they had a healthy fear of Yah and of breaking His Commandments. They also had a *greatness* about them that caused a fear of them in all the city of Jerusalem! They were a *church with Torah!* They kept the Commandments, kept the biblical Feasts and ate clean animals (Leviticus 11). They were not Christians, neither did they know anything about Christianity, Easter, Christmas or Sunday. No, they kept Shabbat and honored Yahveh's Torah. They walked in the Spirit in such glory that even their shadows healed the sick! Anyone that will follow in their footsteps will have the same *greatness* and the same *glory!*

When the snake came to the woman and dismissed the Torah in the Garden as irrelevant, the woman, followed by the man, broke the Commandment and fell into the most horrendous curse! The first event that happens after this, in

Genesis 4, is murder. Cain murders his brother Abel, over the exact same issue! Abel was obeying Elohim's instructions about offerings and sacrifices, but Cain had set up an alternate system and wanted to worship Yah his own way!

**If you do well, will you not be accepted? And if you do not do well, sin lies at the door. And its desire is for you, but you should rule over it.**

Genesis 4:7

In other words, "If you follow My instructions on how to worship Me (*Torah*), then your offering will be accepted and you will be blessed, but if you do 'your own thing, your own way,' disconnected from My Torah Instructions, you will fall into sin. But this doesn't have to happen; I have given you authority over sin!"

When the offering of Abel was accepted and the offering of Cain was not, murder followed! The rejection, diminishing, dismissal and hatred of Torah brings forth murder. Since the divorce of the church from Torah and from the Messianic Jews in 325 AD, during the Council of Nicaea, murder has followed. Millions and millions of Jews have been killed in the name of Christ and this man-made religion called Christianity.

The disciples in the Upper Room on the day of Shavuot were not Christians. They were Jews: followers and disciples of Messiah. They were *great*, they loved Torah, and they were not murderers. In fact, they were martyrs! The gentiles that followed them, such as Cornelius, were *great*. They were lovers of Torah and followers of 'the Way.' They kept the Biblical feasts and they would not have considered breaking the Torah, breaking the Shabbat or eating pork as 'freedom.' (Acts 10)

The rejection, diminishing, dismissal and hatred of Torah brings forth murder.

The acceptance and love of Torah and Yahveh's instructions bring life and *greatness*!

Regarding the Gentiles joining the LORD, this is again confirmed in Isaiah 56:

> "Thus says the LORD: 'Keep justice and do righteousness, for my salvation is about to come, and my righteousness to be revealed.'"
>
> Isaiah 56:1

In other words, in order to prepare for deliverance to come to your life, family, and nation, there needs to be a turning from unrighteousness to righteousness. There has to be a desire to be holy! Repentance precedes deliverance.

> "Blessed is the man who does this, and the son of man who lays hold on it; who keeps from defiling the Sabbath, and keeps his hand from doing any evil."
>
> Isaiah 56:2

In other words, favor, prosperity, and wholeness will follow such a person.

"Do not let the son of the foreigner who has joined himself to Yahveh speak, saying, 'Yahveh has utterly separated me from his people'; nor let the eunuch say, 'Here I am a dry tree.' For thus says the LORD, Yahveh; 'To the eunuchs who keep my Sabbaths, and choose what pleases me, and hold fast my covenant, even to them I will give in my house and within my walls a place and a name better than that of sons and daughters; I will give them an everlasting name that shall not be cut off. Also the sons of the foreigner who join themselves to the LORD, to serve him, and to love the name of the LORD to be his servants – everyone who keeps from defiling the Sabbath, and holds fast my covenant. Even them I will bring to my holy mountain, and make them joyful in my house of prayer. Their burnt offerings and their sacrifices will be accepted on my altar; for my house shall be called a house of prayer for all nations.'"

Isaiah 56:3-7

Great people can talk to the great people of the world such as kings, queens, presidents, and prime ministers. Small people will not be accepted in their presence. All the prophets and apostles of old that loved Yah's Torah were *great*, and so they spoke into the lives of kings and rulers.

Receive the Master's key for greatness – may He make you joyful in His house of prayer and may your offerings be accepted as you follow His Torah by his Spirit of life!

May you become *great* and impact the nations for His glory!

May you become *great*, and like Queen Esther with Mordecai of old, may you rise up and stop satan's plan to bring about another Holocaust to destroy the Jews.

May you become great and be a voice stopping any political programs that want to force Israel to give her land away to her enemies.

May you become *great* as you honor His Word and His Law above everything in your life and as you walk in His Holy Spirit.

May you become *great* as you teach His Torah to others. May you become Great, as He calls you with His glory because of all of the above.

May you become great!

"But whoever does and teaches them shall be called great in the kingdom of heaven."

Matthew 5:19

CHAPTER 10

# Dream SHEEP NATIONS Into Existence

*"Through faith we understand that the worlds were framed by the word of Yah, so that things which are seen were not made of things which do appear."*

— HEBREWS 11:3

Before anyone or anything existed on the *earth*, there was great darkness and great chaos. Then ELOHIM, the Creator God, began *dreaming*. The word in Hebrew says that He formed what He had previously imagined. In fact in Hebrew, the word for "to form" or "to produce and to manifest" is the word, *litsor*, which comes from the word *yetser*, which means "*imagination.*"

*Yetser* is also the word for "inclination and desire" which implies *longing and passion*. *Yetser* is neutral, meaning that the type of manifestation depends on the type of motivation. Because ELOHIM is *love*, the motivation behind all of His thoughts and actions is *love*. In other words, before things manifested in the natural reality of this earth:

Yah loved us and desired us and all of His creation with a longing and a passion. So He dreamt about us and imagined us continually until we came to be!

**In the beginning Elohim created the heavens and the earth. The earth was without form and void; and darkness was on the face of the deep. And the spirit of Elohim was hovering over the face of the waters. Then Elohim said, "let there be light" and there was light.**

Genesis 1:1–3

The Spirit of Elohim, *Ruach Elohim*, is depicted in Hebrew in the female gender. The Spirit was hovering over the waters, like a very protective mother that was nursing and protecting a very sick child. She hovers over him day and night until the child is healed.

So, the Spirit of Elohim is hovering over this very sick world, over all the sick nations, protecting and watching over them. The Spirit of Elohim hovered over you and me before we had the revelation of Messiah which led us to salvation. First the Spirit hovers and then the Word comes. What brings a dream into reality is the Word.

Elohim's word created and continues manifesting everything created into the reality of our senses. The word joins with the Spirit of Elohim like a husband and a wife, and they produce and bring forth life!

We can only understand this mystery through faith. Faith releases divine revelation. When the Word and Spirit of Elohim join, they conceive *life*. Just as when a man and a woman join, they conceive a baby. However, the baby does not manifest her presence until nine months later. You cannot see the baby; it's not out yet, yet you know that the baby exists. It is inside of you and *in the fullness of time the baby will be born so that everyone can see it!*

Today there is a sophisticated technology, called 'ultra-sound' by which we can both see and *take pictures* of a baby while still in the womb. Similarly, Elohim has given us *sophisticated spiritual gifts* through which we can *see, envision and take a picture* of things that are not seen.

Through faith and prophetic revelation, motivated by the love of the Father, Elohim, Yahveh we can see in the spirit realm that there is a 'baby' coming!

- He is bringing Israel forth as His own people and as the Chief Sheep Nation. (Isaiah 2, Isaiah 66:6–24)
- He is hovering over many nations that are without form, void, and in deep darkness.

Since Yeshua came, was sacrificed, rose from the dead, and ascended to heaven, we have become the carriers of Elohim's word and Spirit. We are the ones to bring forth nations into life beginning with the chief of all nations, Israel.

**And Yeshua came and spoke to them saying, "all authority has been given to Me in heaven and on earth. Go therefore and make disciples of all nations, baptizing them (in My name), teaching them to observe all things that I have commanded you; and lo, I am with you always, even to the end of the age."**

Matthew 28:18–20

The Spirit in us, through prayer and worship, begins to hover over a nation, ethnic group, tribe, or region. He begins to manifest the love, care, and protection of ELOHIM. Then we speak the Word, His prophetic, life-giving word – His Torah, His holy Commandments, and precious promises.

And a baby is conceived.

*A Sheep Nation is conceived. A dream is conceived.* A Yah given *dream* is conceived for that nation. Then you let the dream grow. You yield to that dream inside of you and let the dream grow and flow in you until it manifests. Do not choke the dream through unbelief, selfishness or fear. Many mothers choke their babies through their own negative emotions or because they drink, smoke and eat junk foods. And so many babies are born deformed and too small.

In the same way, when you are in unbelief, worry, anxiety and fear, when you 'smoke negativity or self-pity' and 'drink bitterness' and things other than His word, you can cause your own dream within you to either:

1. Die
2. Be born deformed and defective
3. Be born prematurely
4. Be born too small

When I was pregnant with my first born, my daughter Adi, my mother-in-law would tell me about the importance of a 'cow-like attitude' of surrender. In other words: You are pregnant. You are going to lose your present shape, and you are going to grow. Now relax, and let it happen!

To this I will add the importance of: talking to your baby, dreaming about and massaging it, imagining it until it manifests. Parents begin to imagine what the baby will look like – will it be a boy or a girl?

Also, by faith they begin designing the baby's room and they *engage their finances in preparing for the baby on the way.* It is also very important to have an exercise plan for an easier pregnancy and delivery.

So as you conceive a dream for a nation to be *born again as a Sheep Nation* through the "Key of Abraham" described in this book, begin to:
1. Surrender to the dream
2. Talk the Word to it
3. Massage it with your love and prayers
4. Feed it with positive attitudes of faith
5. Engage your finances in preparing for the Sheep Nation to be born.
6. Exercise your faith and take important steps guided by the Holy Spirit as you prepare for that Day.

Just like a pregnancy takes over the life of that expectant couple, so it is when you conceive any dream from Yah, especially the dream of a Sheep Nation. You need not fear that this dream will take over your entire life! Remember: Fear causes babies to be born defective: emotionally or physically. So do not fear. Perfect love casts out all fear. Just feed your dream in prayer and with the Word.

Is there a nation in your heart? Have you been 'hovering over it' in your thoughts and prayers? Maybe you have been afraid to even think that you can birth an entire nation and/or region? Let the dream grow! But let your dream be based on Elohim's Word!

Now I am going to be dreaming before you about the chief nation – Israel. All the other nations need to follow the lead or chief sheep. As you dream about Israel and put it first in your dreaming, you will be able to form the right kind of dream for every other nation in the world and that particular 'baby' that Yah is giving to you!

Then you shall say unto Pharaoh, "Thus says the LORD, Israel is My son, My firstborn."

Exodus 4:22

The firstborn carries the blessing of authority and a double portion! The firstborn is always considered the *leader of the family*. Israel is the *leader of the nations*. Now you can understand why such a tiny piece of Land, such a small nation, can command so much publicity and media attention from the world. Israel has a calling to be the leader of the nations!

Since Israel, as a nation, is Yah's firstborn Sheep Nation, it follows that He also has other nations that are not his firstborn, yet they are His children!

Let me give you an example that will surprise you:

> In that day there will be a highway from Egypt to Assyria, and the Egyptians will serve with the Assyrians. In that day Israel will be one of the three with Egypt and Assyria – a blessing in the midst of the land, whom the LORD of hosts shall bless saying, "Blessed is Egypt My people, and Assyria the work of My hands, and Israel My inheritance."

Isaiah 19:23–25

It is clear from this passage that the Assyrians (the area of Iraq and Iran today!) and the Egyptians will be Sheep Ethnos! How will that happen? Just like at the time of creation and just like at the time of Jonah: the Spirit of ELOHIM will hover, is already hovering, over these nations through the prayers, fasting, and worship of some of His holy vessels and priests. Then a

Jonah-type apostolic, prophetic ministry will preach the word of repentance to these nations, and they will repent!

But the message that will be given to these nations must be "the Key of Abraham."

Thus says the LORD: "Against all My evil neighbors who touch the inheritance which I have caused My people Israel to inherit – Behold I will pluck them out of their land and pluck out the house of Judah from among them. Then it shall be after I have plucked them out, that I will return and have compassion on them and bring them back, everyone to his heritage and everyone to his land. And it shall be, If they will learn carefully the ways of My people, (Torah!), to swear by My name (Yahveh-Yeshua not Allah!), 'As the LORD lives' as they taught My people to swear by Baal, then they shall be established in the midst of My people. But if they do not obey (Torah!), I will utterly pluck up and destroy that nation" says the LORD."

Jeremiah 12:14–17

If such wicked, anti-Jewish, anti-Israel nations such as Iraq, Iran and Egypt can be saved and become SHEEP NATIONS by obeying Yah's Torah, we can conclude that many other nations less wicked can also be saved and become SHEEP NATIONS if they follow the principle of 'The Key of Abraham!'

This is why I have hope for such wicked nations as Germany, France, Chile and 'neutral' Switzerland. But nothing will happen unless we begin dreaming the Word, massaging it with prayer and worship, and nourishing it with acts of faith.

Let me tell you that dreaming is fun. It brings joy, hope, expectation, and excitement. A spirit of legalism and religion kills dreams, but a spirit of faith will let the dreams flow until they manifest!

Joseph, the beloved son of Jacob, was a dreamer. It was his dream that kept him hopeful even in the worst of circumstances. He was thrown into the pit by his brothers, was falsely accused, and put in jail. Still he never let the dream die. I believe that he let that dream overtake his life and circumstances until that dream's presence became stronger than any adverse circumstances and hindrances! And finally His dream came to pass!

Yah-given dreams are not a way of escaping a painful reality. Dreams that originate with and are given by Yah are the way to reform reality until it matches His will, longing, and desire.

**Your Kingdom come; Your will be done on earth as it is in heaven.**

**Matthew 6:10**

Only dreamers can bring heaven down to earth! The holy Scriptures are full of dreamers that have shaped the history of the world. These faith dreamers (and they are all Israelis) are mentioned in Hebrews 11:32–33:

**And what more shall I say? For the time would fail me to tell of Gideon, and Barak and Samson, and Jephthah, also of David, Samuel and the prophets: Who through faith subdued kingdoms, worked righteousness, obtained promises, stopped the mouths of lions…**

**Hebrews 11:32–33**

As we follow in the steps of our Israeli forefathers, beginning with Abraham, we too will subdue kingdoms and bring His Kingdom down on many nations!

Most of the church has had an escape mentality. They are waiting for the 'Rapture' to happen. So their 'dream' is to get out of here! But that is not a Yah-given dream because, you see, even after you 'get out of here,' you will be coming back to reign (if you have followed Messiah's ways!) with Him for one thousand years, and His throne will be in Jerusalem! Besides that, after the millennial reign of Messiah on earth, the New Heavens and the New Earth, the New Jerusalem will *come down,* right here to *this* earth and to *this* Israel.

Listen well. Yah is not a destroying God, He is a *restoring* and *redeeming* God! He did not send Yeshua to destroy His creation but rather to redeem it. That includes all the nations, all the earth!

Please stop escaping and begin to dream some Sheep Nations into existence. Begin to dream Israel *fully* redeemed, and then nations, many nations, that will follow her example.

Ezekiel dreamt of a great restoration of Israel, of a Mighty Army that came out of a valley full of dry bones. That was over 2500 years ago and the people of Israel *together* with the grafted in, born again believers from the Gentiles are becoming a Mighty Army to reckon with! (Ezekiel 37)

Begin to dream and see in the eyes of the Spirit those nations that He wants to put in your heart, and then massage it with the Word and prayer. You will never be the same, and the nations will never be the same!

Look what it says about Israel and the nations:

"Who has heard of such a thing? Who has seen such things? Shall the earth be made to give birth in one day? Or shall a nation be born at once? For as soon as Zion was in labor, she gave birth to her children."

Isaiah 66:8

When you massage a Yah-given dream, all of a sudden it happens! The 'suddenlies' of Yah are preceded by a lot of dreaming and faith actions!

Now Zion is the mother of many children! Zion is another name for Jerusalem, Israel, the Land of Israel, and the people of Israel. In other words Zion, Israel, is the mother of many children! She is being called to be the lead Sheep Nation, and to give birth to many other SHEEP NATIONS!

**Rejoice with Jerusalem and be glad with her, all you who love her; rejoice for joy with her, all you who mourn for her. That you may feed and be satisfied with the consolation of her bosom, that you may drink deeply and be satisfied with the abundance of her glory. For thus says the LORD: "Behold I will extend to her peace like a river, and the glory of the gentiles like a flowing stream. Then you shall feed; on her sides shall you be carried, and be dandled on her knees."**

Isaiah 66:10–12

Israel, the chief nation, will dandle the other SHEEP NATIONS as children on her knees, and they will be comforted and blessed!

Come on begin dreaming...

FORECLOSURE

# End Word

This ending was given to me by the Holy Spirit, and I am fully aware now of what it means. Yeshua is taking His house, the church, back!

In order to turn nations into SHEEP NATIONS, Yah is in need of people with greatness – humble but great. And only obedience makes us great.

I am fully aware that you, your family, your church, and your community need to undergo a revolution and that you need more information about Torah and the Feasts. While there are some books out, especially in English and German, they are missing in almost every other language. There is no doubt that as this move of Yah advances, there will be much more material available. However, I believe that the LORD wants you to connect with Messianic apostolic Jews that can teach you Torah and help you. The move is young, and we are not many, but our number is growing. We, personally, cannot come to disciple every church in every nation. However, we are committed to travel and to come to key communities and to key leadership, both of the church, the nation and the business communities. We have a special burden to disciple business leaders into the blessing of Abraham, as you are called to finance the End time gospel, and to help turn many nations into SHEEP NATIONS.

If you are a key person in your area who can organize an Apostolic Convention on the topic of "the Blessing of Abraham" and "Turning your nation into a Sheep Nation," by all means contact us at the address on page 146 or by e-mail, info@kadesh.org. Please do not fail to contact us. You are very *important* for the End time plan of Yah.

Even if you are a small community, contact us. We will try to help you either by coming personally or by connecting you with another apostolic Messianic Jew that can. Do not think that you are too small as it takes one or two in obedience to turn a nation around.

APPENDIX 1

# 2017 Anti-semitism Report

The following article is a report from 2017 posted on *The Coordination Forum for Countering Antisemitism*, an official Israeli government site monitoring Antisemitism throughout the world:

## General

According to the Report published by the Coordination Forum for Countering Antisemitism there has been an increase in the number of anti-Semitic incidents and violent attacks against Jews.

The Islamic anti-Semitism continues to be the main and most dangerous threat to the Jewish communities and it has been this Islamic anti-Semitism which inspired the murder of Sarah Halimi in Paris on April 5, 2017. Incitement by radical Islamic states and institutions continued also this year and legitimated attacks against Jews.

# ISLAMIC ANTISEMITISM

## Introduction

The last two decades there has been an increase in the role of Islamic radicals in the instigation of anti-Semitism in Western Europe. If in the past various neo-Nazi groups and the radical left have been the main source of anti-Semitism, in recent years it turns out that the instigators of most anti-Semitic incidents in Europe are mainly Europeans of Muslim origin who in some cases even mentioned their interpretation of Islam to justify their actions.

The situation of anti-Semitism in the Arab World remained unchanged compared to last year. When the subject of Israel or an issue perceived as Israeli or Zionist was raised, such as the Temple Mount, the 100th anniversary of the Balfour Declaration, discussions on the status of holy sites in UNESCO and recently President Trump's decision to recognize Jerusalem as the capital of Israel, an anti-Semitic outburst followed almost immediately in Arab countries and among Muslim audiences around the world.

Antisemitic incitement was led by official institutions and spokesmen of states, civil organizations and religious organizations. They used frequent and extensive anti-Semitic narratives together with motifs of classic Christian anti-Semitism, Nazi racialism and new anti-Semitism, in order to foster hatred and demonize and dehumanize Jews and Israel.

These motifs also echoed in broadcasted and written media, where the Jews were described as being corrupt, greedy, scheming and trouble-makers who try to take over the world and harm humanity.

## Iran: the leading country in its support of anti-Semitism

The trends that have characterized the Iranian regime in recent years have continued in 2017. Despite the fact that Iran does not share a border with Israel and has never been in a territorial dispute with Israel, it continues to be a major player in the anti-Semitic incitement, which calls for wiping Israel off the map and promoting anti-Semitic and Holocaust denial.

Iran's supreme leader Ayatollah Ali Khamenei said in February that the State of Israel was a "fake state" and that it was a "dirty chapter" in history. Khamenei's speech was delivered at a pro-Palestinian conference held in Tehran once every four years.

## FAR RIGHT

### Far Right in the United States

The violent acts that took place in Charlottesville, Virginia highlighted the rise of the extreme right-wing organizations in the country. They protested under the slogan "unite the right" and shouted harsh words against Jews. These are organizations whose roots are deeply embedded in American history, and are often characterized by anti-Semitic, neo-Nazi, racist and nationalist ideology. Lately they have been gaining strength and they are more powerful than they have been for years.

According to SPLC, the Alabama-based Southern Poverty Law Center, there are no fewer than 917 extremist groups - racist, hate organizations and extremist militias, a steep rise from 784 three years ago when 99 were classified as neo-Nazi, 130 as the KKK racist movement, 78 as racist skinhead organizations, and 100 nationalist organizations advocating white supremacy.

## The KKK (Ku Klux Klan)

The KKK is the largest and most known group in the United States. It was founded 150 years ago, in 1865, by officers from the southern states who fought in the civil war that broke out in 1860 in the name of the Confederate States and the right of those states to separate from the United States and to decide for themselves on policies such as the preservation of slavery.

The organization initially succeeded in the Southern states and spread throughout the US during the 20th century. The affiliates promoted discrimination against blacks, Jews and immigrants, and later against LGBT. The KKK has become an organization aimed at preventing these groups from enjoying the same civil rights as the rest of the Americans.

The Ku Klux Klan is active in almost 50 states throughout the United States, and according to the "Alabama-based Southern Poverty Law Center " they count between 5,000 and 8,000 members.

## Neo-Nazi organizations

In the United States, various neo-Nazi organizations share anti-Semitic ideologies and admiration for Adolf Hitler and Nazi Germany and some even participated in demonstrations in Virginia. The Neo-Nazi viewpoints are protected by the courts and the First Amendment, which guarantee absolute freedom of expression. In one known case, the Supreme Court approved a neo-Nazi march in the Jewish neighborhood of Skokie, Illinois, during which swastikas were displayed. The prominent neo-Nazi organizations active today are the American Nazi Party and the National Socialist Movement, founded in 1994. Their members wore armlets with swastikas during demonstrations, but recently stopped displaying Nazi symbols in an attempt to increase the influence.

The most popular neo-Nazi organization is the "National Alliance". One of the organizations that split from this organization, "Vanguard America," took part in the parade "Unite the Right" in Virginia.

In 2011, the National Alliance counted 400 members and in 2012 the number was estimated at 2500. But the organizations gained influence in recent years and spread to more regions. Members of the National Socialist Movement are active in 32 different countries.

## Europe's far right

The extreme right-wing parties in Europe were not able to win the national elections in 2017, but extreme right-wing parties in Europe have been very successful in 2017.

Since 2015 more than 1.5 million people have reached the shores of Europe, many of them fleeing the civil war in Syria. The resentment towards those immigrants and the disappointment from their government, was particularly high among the German and Austrian population. In those two countries in the European Union, the number of asylum seekers being accepted into the country, has been the highest.

The Eurosceptic parties promoted an agenda against immigrants and their historic results in the last elections show that their narrative has been successful. As a result, the far right in Europe is more popular today than at any period in post-war history.

## Radical Left

Compared to radical right populist parties (talking to a public of common people to raise support and sympathy, using simple and catchy messages) who see the threat to national identity in their countries and want to neutralize the Jewish influence, the populist parties of the extreme left link the Jews to cosmopolitan elite and world capitalism against which they are fighting.

In this context, attention must be paid to the alliance between the radical left and radical Islam – two groups with worldviews that do not seem compatible - but cooperate against Israel and the Jews. This strange alliance is explained by a new theory called "Intersectionality" (intersection of oppression) adopted by many in the extreme left, calling for the intersection of all discriminated groups. The basis for this theory is the union of all those groups who feel themselves discriminated and deprived, to fight together against their enemies separately.

People who represent radical Islam today have succeeded in unifying their hatred towards Israel. They present their hatred as being a genuine concern for Palestinian rights. They are in favor for intersectionality, while portraying Israel as a daemon that all people must fight. They are doing everything in their power to inculcate anti-Semitic ideas into the mainstream discourse. This discourse paints Israeli Jews as white tyrants (in contrast to the opinion of the extreme right-wing anti-Semites, who view the Jews as an inferior race) while Muslims in general and Palestinians in particular are seen as part of the oppressed and deprived in the world.

The alliance between the radical left and radical Islam is destructive, because students face a clear choice: support for Israel, which provokes ostracism from left-wing circles and human rights organizations, or joining the anti-Israel and anti-Semitic campaign.

Extremists and radical leftists create an alternative reality, according to which Jews have no right to self determination and Israel is the greatest violator of human rights in the world.

## THE NEW ANTISEMITISM

## Definition

The new anti-Semitism includes Islamic anti-Semitic, Christian, Catholic and modern aspects that emerged at the end of the 20th century and became stronger in the early 21st century. In contrast to the traditional expressions of anti-Semitism in which they sought to create a reality where only one truth prevails while eliminating the other, the new anti-Semitism seeks to recognize the other while respecting cultural, ethnic and religious diversity while excluding Israel as a rogue society that clings to Zionism as an ethnocentric model of a nation-state. The new anti-Semitism is characterized by hatred and incitement against the State of Israel and opposes its existence, alongside hatred and violence against Jews.

## BDS - Boycott, Divestment, Sanctions

One of the political manifestations of the new phenomenon of anti-Semitism is the BDS movement. The conference in Durban, South Africa, in 2001 has formed the roots of the BDS movement by defining Israel as an apartheid state. The participants of the conference called for the isolation of Israel and the adoption of international sanctions against it. The decision of the Durban conference was the basis for the establishment of BDS Movement, launched officially in July 2005.

The BDS movement hierarchy consists of dozens of non-governmental organizations and extremist activists working to achieve a common goal. The activity of the movement is funded largely by the generous donations from foreign governments, organizations and companies, religious institutions and private donors.

## Antisemitism on social networks

Social networks are responsible for the global rise in verbal abuse over the past year. The discourse there has become more and more violent, reflecting hatred of Jews (and other minorities).

Also in other European countries there has been an increase in the amount of hate speech on Internet. Many media sites including Facebook and Twitter already have site policies or laws prohibiting incitement, harassment and abusive behavior. But the rise in incitement this year raises questions about the role played by social or technological media in responding to online incitement.

Since social networks have become a leading platform for the spreading of anti-Semitic hate content, social and governmental activities are becoming increasingly important in order to create clearer rules regarding the publication of offensive content on social networks. More efforts should be done by the internet companies in order to locate and remove anti-Semitic content.

# REVIEW BY COUNTRIES

## France

According to a report by the Interior Ministry, in 2017 there was a decrease in racist incidents, including vandalism and physical attacks, despite an increase in violence against Jews and Muslims.

Violent incidents against minorities increased from 67 to 72 against Muslims and from 77 to 97 against Jews.

For the first time since 2008, attacks on religious sites have declined by a total of 7.5% compared to 2016.

Christian sites saw a drop of 7.5% and 878 incidents and attacks on Muslim sites dropped by 15% to 72 incidents.

However, there was a sharp increase of 22 percent in the number of attacks on Jewish sites - although their numbers were relatively low.

# Britain

The CST Antisemitic Incidents Report 2017 shows that CST has recorded 1,382 anti-Semitic incidents in 2017, the highest number ever recorded by the CST for a single calendar year, an increase of 3% from 1,346 recorded incidents during 2016, which itself was an annual peak. The previous peak was in 2014, when CST recorded 1,182 anti-Semitic incidents.

In addition to the 1,382 anti-Semitic incidents, the CST reported another 872 incidents that were potentially anti-Semitic but not included in the report because the CST believes that cannot be defined as anti-Semitic. Most of these 872 incidents are related to suspicious activity or hostile visits to Jewish places, criminal activity affecting Jews, anti-Israeli activity which didn't include anti-Semitic language or motivation.

The high numbers throughout 2017 continued the pattern of 2016 and occurred by a combination of factors, including an increase in all types of hate crimes and publication of alleged anti-Semitism in the Labor Party. These factors may lead to higher numbers of incidents as well as encourage people in the Jewish community to report anti-Semitic incidents. This differs from previous peaks in 2014 and 2009, when military confrontations between Israel and Hamas in Gaza served as a one-time accelerator for peaks in the number of incidents.

In total, more than 100 anti-Semitic incidents were recorded from January to October 2017, after 19 consecutive months in which more than 100 incidents were recorded every month. By comparison, monthly summaries alone exceeded 100 monthly incidents in six cases in the ten years preceding April 2016.

## Antisemitism within the Labor Party

The Labor Party led by Corbin increased its number of representatives in the parliament from 232 seats to 266 in the 2017 elections and became the second largest party in the British parliament. Many members of the Jewish community were concerned about these results following Corbin's statements and those of the party members and their supporters in the past. At an event during the Labor conference in Brighton, there were a number of anti-Semitic and anti-Israel / Zionist incidents indicating the party's growing radicalization.

At the event anti-Zionist activists compared Israel to the Nazi regime, accusing it of committing "genocide" in the Gaza Strip. In addition, several deputies and members of parliament called for "kicking" pro-Israel organizations from the Labor party while referring to the Jewish Labor Organization and the Friends of Israel in the Labor Party.

## Germany

After a three-year decline in the number of anti-Semitic incidents, there has been an increase in 2017 in the number of anti-Semitic incidents in Germany following the refugee and immigrant crisis and the strengthening of the right-wing nationalists.

A study by the Amadeu Antonio Stiftung about anti-Semitic trends in Germany shows that classical anti-Semitism, motivated by Christian motives and stereotypes of Jews as the killers of Jesus, is giving way to new types of anti-Semitism, such as anti-Semitism linked to Israel and secondary anti-Semitism (historical relativism and Holocaust denial).

From those findings we can conclude three important conclusions regarding anti-Semitism in Germany:

- Agreeing with classic forms of anti-Semitism has been diminishing in recent years in Germany.

- Instead, Germans express their anti-Semitism in an indirect way, usually in the form of anti-Semitic statements referring to the State of Israel (anti-Semitism related to the State of Israel)

- Antisemitic phenomena appear in waves. Sometimes the number of anti-Semitic incidents decreases, and then it rises again. But one cannot deduce from this the opposite conclusion that anti-Semitism itself once declines and then rises. On the contrary, anti-Semitism is always latent in society and can be mobilized at any time. The public discussion is less about the hatred of Jews from the democratic center than the hatred from right wing extremists or Muslim communities. While according to studies on mesenteric attitudes in society, the "classical" anti-Semitism has been losing support for years, anti-Semitism associated with Israel belongs to the main forms of modern anti-Semitism. This form is often expressed indirectly. The anti-Semitism of the democratic center is expressed by way of indirect communication. It is precisely those subtle forms of anti-Semitism that pose a danger to democratic values and social life, because they are usually not felt and thus become the norm.

## Australia – data from the Executive Council of Australian Jews (ECAJ)

According to Australia's annual report on anti-Semitism published by the Australian Jewish Leadership Council (ECAJ), there has been an increase of 9.5% in the number of anti-Semitic incidents in Australia in the last 12 months ending September 30, 2017 including threats or acts of violence.

The ECAJ, the umbrella organization of the Jewish community in each country, recorded a total of 230 anti-Semitic incidents during this period, including physical attacks, abuse and harassment, vandalism, graffiti, hate messages and threats received directly by e-mail, letters, telephone calls, and flyers compared to 210 such cases recorded by the same sources during the previous 12 months.

145 incidents including attacks (assault, abuse, vandalism and graffiti) accounted for 63% of all incidents, and 85 incidents including threats (e-mail, letters, phone calls, newsletters) accounted for 37% of all incidents. There are also oral testimonies concerning not registered events.

Overall, the number of "attacks" remained unchanged, while the rate of "threats" increased by 39% between 2016 and 2017. There was a significant increase in anti-Semitic graffiti and posters and a decrease in the number of attacks and vandalism, as well as a slight decrease in the number of harassments.

"The most striking change in the past 12 months in Australia is the increase in extreme right-wing activity" said Julie Nathan, ECAJ Research Director, who focused mainly on the activities of a small neo-Nazi group, Antipodean Resistance, created in October 2016. The group was founded in Melbourne but has now branches in most other countries. Its activities have focused on pasting thousands of Nazi stickers and thousands of anti-Jewish, anti-gay and pro-Nazi posters, mostly at universities and elsewhere.

This aroused great concern among the Jewish communities. Some of the group's posters express support for violence and murder, calling for "the legalization of the execution of Jews" and the killing of homosexuals by shooting them in their heads.

## USA

New data released by the Anti-Defamation League show that the number of anti-Semitic incidents in 2017 is higher than last year. In addition to the significant increase during the first quarter of the year, there was also a clear increase after the right-wing march in Charlottesville in August.

According to the organization's latest "Audit Report on Antisemitic Incidents," there were 1,299 anti-Semitic incidents across the United States between January 1 and September 30 that included physical attacks, property destruction and attacks on Jewish institutions. The total number of incidents represents a 67% increase for the same period last year and is already higher than the total reported incidents over the past year. A very alarming number of anti-Semitic incidents and anti-Semitic property destruction were recorded in schools and college campuses throughout the United States.

Compared to 2016, there was a higher number of incidents in each of the first three quarters of 2017. These number of incidents peaked in the first quarter of 2017 and slowed somewhat down in the second and third quarters. Out of the 1,299 anti-Semitic incidents recorded so far in 2017, the majority (667) occurred in the first quarter of the year. 632 additional anti-Semitic incidents were reported in the second and third quarters of the year, more than the 488 incidents reported during the same period last year.

According to the report the number of reported incidents in primary and secondary schools in 2017 doubled compared to the same period last year (269 incidents compared to 130 in 2016), and 142 incidents of harassment and 114 incidents of vandalism were registered. In universities 118 anti-Semitic incidents were reported in the first three quarters of 2017, compared to 74 incidents in the same period last year - an increase of 59%.

## The Former Soviet Union (written with the help of Native Prime Minister's office)

While in 2016 there has been a significant decrease in anti-Semitic incidents in the former Soviet Union, 2017 was marked by an increase in the number of incidents, mainly in Ukraine.

As in previous years, the number of violent incidents (assaults, threats, and harassment) remained low, except for a certain increase in the number of threats and calls in Ukraine to attack Jews. It is important to note that the number of anti-Semitic incidents in the former Soviet Union does not generally reflect the true severity of anti-Semitism. Therefore, it is very important to examine the essence of the trends in depth.

The national anti-Semitism in the former Soviet Union is almost not existing. Jews can practice their religious rites unhindered and there are no restrictions on education or employment. Still, there are elements, mainly in Russia and the Ukraine, who use anti-Semitic content, usually only verbal, for their own purposes as they serve the immediate political and public needs of those individuals.

The trends characterizing the countries did not change significantly in 2017: in Russia there are publications representing the Jews as foreign and hostile elements as opposed to Ukraine, where there is vandalism against Jewish sites, use of anti-Semitism for political aims and an increased preoccupation with the Ukrainian national historical memory, part of which involves harming the Jewish population.

## Russia

As in previous years, the number of incidents decreased in 2017. The main manifestations of anti-Semitism concentrated on a number of major historical-cultural issues: the Bolshevik Revolution of 1917, the collapse of the Soviet Union in 1991 and the "wild capitalism" of the 1990s. Not only were the Jews seen as the motivating factors in all these events, but also as the main beneficiaries, who established their wealth and status over the suffering of the Russian people. The year 2017, which marked the 100th anniversary of the Bolshevik Revolution, also featured a series of articles, movies and documentaries emphasizing in a negative way the role of the Jews in those events.

## Ukraine

For the second consecutive year, Ukraine is at the head of the countries with the largest number of anti-Semitic incidents in the former Soviet Union, with an emphasis on anti-Semitic propaganda in political discourse and vandalism against Jewish sites: cemeteries, memorial sites for Holocaust victims and community buildings have been attacked. As in previous years, even in 2017, the lack of organized activity by the authorities to prevent anti-Semitic incidents led to the phenomenon of "repeated desecration," where Jewish sites are consistently affected time after time, without the authorities doing anything to stop this. Moreover, in many cases, anti-Semitic incidents are classified as "hooliganism" and are not dealt with at all. Therefore, it is not inconceivable that there are also events, some of which may even be violent, which did not reach the media. It should be noted, however, that not only the Jews but also members of other ethnic minorities fall victim to nationalistic incidents, but the high incidence of incidents against the Jews makes them the most prominent among all hate events in the country. Following the "Revolution of Dignity" in early 2014, it seems that Ukraine, which once stood out for the use of anti-Semitic content for political purposes, managed to leave this behind.

In the last two years, however, the use of the "Jewish card" in the political and public discourse in Ukraine has not only increased, but has even become more common. While post-revolution public figures of Jewish origin were appointed to senior positions in the new government, nowadays the Jewishness of these people is perceived as one of the causes of the difficult socio-political situation in the country. Moreover, even non-Jewish leaders are perceived by the people as "hidden Jews." In the past, however, only extreme supporters of Eastern separatists or nationalists in the West made such claims, including politicians and other public figures.

Under the auspices of the Institute, official ceremonies are celebrated and authorities and citizens are called upon to pay homage to those who "fight the people who tried to enslave the people of Ukraine". However, some of these national heroes not only encouraged the abuse of the Jewish population but also played an active role in its eradication. All this lead to a great antagonism over the Jewish issue of glorifying national heroes when one side glorifies the national heroes and the other side accuses the glorification of the murderers while at the same time ignoring the role of the local population in the murder of the Jews. This phenomenon does not relate only to World War II. The attacks on the Jews during the short period of Ukrainian independence after the revolution in 1917 became an issue in the relations between Jewish organizations and the Ukrainian establishment. Responses to Jewish protests who came mostly from the nationalist elements, included calls to expel the Jews from the Ukraine or, at the very least, to remind them of who owned the country. There were also those who claimed that harming the Jews was a legitimate act because the involvement of the Jews in the attack on the Ukrainian people, especially the starvation (HOLODOMOR) in 1932-1933, without mentioning, that Jewish citizens also fell victim to the same starvation.

## DEFINITION OF ANTISEMITISM

The traditional definition of anti-Semitism - "hostility toward or discrimination against Jews as a religious, ethnic or social group" - corresponds to the classic religious anti-Semitism of Christianity in the Middle Ages and the nationalist anti-

Semitism of the Nazis. But this definition is not suitable for the new contemporary anti-Semitism.

Britain adopted the "Working Definition of Antisemitism," due to an increase in anti-Semitic incidents and because the struggle against prejudices towards Jews is an important part is of its efforts to build a fairer society.

This is a practical definition which is not interested in the identity and motives of the anti-Semites and not in the way they see the Jews. It states, in one sentence, that anti-Semitism is a certain perception of Jews, accompanied by hatred feelings toward them, which are translated into verbal violence against them, their communities and their institutions. And finally, examples of statements against Israel which are considered anti-Semitic such as the denial of the Jewish people's right to self-determination, the use of symbols and anti-Semitic imagery, comparing Israeli citizens to the Nazis and discussing its policy in a discriminatory way.

Contemporary examples of anti-Semitism in public life, the media, schools, workplaces and religious spaces can include the following - though not exclusively:

- Reading, helping or justifying the killing or harming of Jews in the name of a radical ideology or in the name of a radical religious vision.

- References that deny Jews their humanity, demonize them or attribute them stereotypes as individuals or as a group - as though not exclusively the myth of a global Jewish plot to control the media, the economy, the government, or other institutions of society

- Accusing Jews as nation, of being responsible for negative actions, real or imagined, committed by a single Jewish person or a group, or even for acts committed by non-Jews.

- Denial of the existence, purpose and mechanisms (eg. gas-chambers) of the extermination of the Jewish people by Nazi Germany, its supporters and allies during the Second World War.

- Accusing the Jews as a nation or Israel as a state, of inventing or exaggerating the Holocaust's dimensions.

- Accusing Jewish citizens who do not live in Israel, of being more loyal to Israel, or favoring Jewish interests worldwide over the interests of the state in which they live.

- Examples of the ways in which anti-Semitism can be expressed in relation to the State of Israel may include:

- Denying the Jewish people's right to self-determination, inter alia, by claiming that the existence of Israel is a racist endeavor.

- Applying double standards towards Israel, demanding that it acts in a manner that is not expected or required of any other democratic nation.

- Using the symbols and images associated with classic anti-Semitism (eg. the claim that the Jews killed Jesus, or blood libel) to characterize Israel or Israelis.

- Comparison of contemporary Israeli policy to that of the Nazis.

- Collective vision of the Jews as responsible for Israel's actions.

However, criticism of Israel similar to that leveled against any other country cannot be regarded as anti-Semitic.

Antisemitic acts are criminal when they are defined as such by law (for example, as defined in some countries: Holocaust denial or anti-Semitic propaganda). Criminal acts are anti-Semitic when the targets of attacks, whether people or property, such as buildings, schools, places of worship and cemeteries, are chosen by the attackers because they are, or are perceived as Jewish or linked to Jews. Antisemitic discrimination is preventing equal opportunity for Jews. (CFCA)

For more information to become aware of anti-Semitic acts in your particular nation, please visit: www.antisemitism.org.il

APPENDIX 2

# Two Weddings and One Divorce

Why is it so urgent to bring this information?
- Yahveh is a holy God.
- Anti-Semitism is rising to alarming proportions throughout the world.
- Satan wants to destroy Israel through the Palestinian Issue.
- Archbishop Dominiquae was visited by the LORD in Chile when He showed her that after 2,000 years of gospel, there was *not one* nation that He could call a 'sheep nation' according to Matthew 25:32.
- Satan wants to destroy all the nations by influencing them to hate God's Torah (Laws and precepts) and to hate the Jewish people and the State of Israel. (See Isaiah 34, Obadiah, Zechariah 12, Psalms 83)
- The church is supposed to disciple nations. Matthew 28:19
- The church has to change and return to the Jewish/biblical roots and retrieve the gospel that the Jewish apostles preached.
Prophecy from Lance Lambert:

"My anger is stirred up, says the LORD, against the nations for they are dividing My land and seeking to destroy *my* heritage. My furious anger is like a boiling cauldron against those powerful states that have produced such strategies and who by pressure and manipulation are seeking to implement them. Now, I will become their enemy, says the LORD, and I will judge them with natural disasters, by physical catastrophes, by fire, by flood, by earthquakes, and by eruptions. I will touch the seas, the atmosphere, the earth and all that is within them. Moreover, I will touch them where it will hurt them the most for I will touch their power and the foundations of affluence and prosperity. I will smash their prosperous economies, says the LORD. And I will overturn, and overturn, and overturn that they may know that I am the LORD." (CFI-USA)

*The Holocaust and the Christian World* by Ritner, Smith & Steinfeldt:

"Many Christians when confronted with the Shoa (Nazi Holocaust), gaze on it as if some aliens landed on the earth, took the name 'Nazi' and proceeded to torture and kill Jews. They regard the perpetrators of these monstrous acts as from another planet, as people that otherwise did not hug their children, weep at the death of a parent, bleed when they were wounded – in other words, non-human creatures without a conscience, automatons of some mad and evil creator. But the Shoa (Holocaust) is not the story about a group of alien people, rather about human beings. And they, we must admit, were primarily Christians, from the great Lutheran and Catholic tradition. Somehow they had lost that which made them followers of Jesus or they had chosen to suppress it in their horrid pursuit of killing Jews." (Ritner, Smith and Steinfeldt)

## Two Weddings and One Divorce

The following illustration will explain why Christianity was 'the womb' of the Spanish Inquisition, the Crusades, and the Nazi Holocaust. Yahveh-God is looking to the church for repentance in order to influence the nations and fulfill the mandate of Matthew 28:19 *"Go and make disciples of all nations."*

The first and original church was married to a Jewish Husband by the name of Yeshua the Messiah & into His family the Jewish people (Ephesians 2:14 and Romans 11). The Wedding Ceremony took place in Jerusalem. It was ratified and sealed by the spilling of the blood of the Husband and by the breaking of His body. (Luke 22:15–20) The time of this marriage was the holy biblical Feast of Passover. The fruit of this miraculous wedding was thousands and thousands of people, both Jews and Gentiles, saved and healed. Even the shadow of this holy bride healed the sick, as signs and wonders and miracles followed her wherever she went in the name of her Husband Yeshua.

This marriage led the wife to much suffering. Many in the world did not love her Husband and tried to kill her by persecuting her and even throwing her to the lions during the Roman Empire's reign of terror. Those were hard years. After many years of suffering, Yeshua's wife had become weary. He had gone to prepare a place for her and had not come back yet.

She started to get tired from her lifestyle as an outcast, persecuted and hunted at every corner. She longed for peace at any price. She longed for the warm embrace of a Husband who would provide her with peace and security here on this earth... At her weakest point an earthly king appeared. (Matthew 10:34, John 14:27, Jeremiah 8:11)

This earthly king was influential and powerful by earthly standards. He could stop the killing and persecution against her. He could give her the security she longed for... *If* only she would agree to divorce this Jewish Husband of hers and completely separate from His family Israel, and from that Book that she treasured so much – where He had left her all of His instructions and the family legacy of God's Word.

This powerful king seemed to be a spiritual man. He claimed that her Jewish Husband had appeared to him in a dream and had given him the crown of the Roman Empire. His deceptive charm and appeasing manners managed to attract the very weary bride of Messiah, but not all were deceived. There was a portion of the bride/church/ecclesia that was not fooled by the charms of this deceitful king. These were the Messianic Jews of the time.

They were too rooted in the writings of the Holy Book and the ancient Hebrew Scriptures to be deceived. But the vast majority of the believers at that time were Gentiles, and they did not want any more suffering on behalf of the Book, its Author, or His family.

They wanted freedom and peace at all cost.

The powerful Constantine sang the song of peace and safety and prepared a bed of roses... The Gentile portion of the church slept with him, falling into violent adultery and wounding the heart of her heavenly Jewish Husband. In order to appease the conscience of this adulterous church, Constantine decided to legalize this unholy union in the year AD 325 by means of a wedding ceremony called the Council of Nicaea and drawing up an ungodly and illegal marriage contract called the Nicean Creed.

He used his worldly power to draw all the gentile church fathers, which for the most part were already anti-Semitic and hated their Jewish roots. These church fathers were to be witnesses of this horrendous divorce and the adulterous new marriage between the predominantly Gentile church and another Jesus, a product of Constantine's own creation.

This alternative Savior came with another family, another book (totally disconnected from the ancient Hebrew writings), other customs, Laws, festivals, traditions and ways of measuring time.

Knowing that his brand-new wife was accustomed to worshipping God, he organized for her a god that would suit her perfectly by not demanding any holiness from her. He presented a god of peace that was lenient towards a mixture of paganism and holiness: An all-inclusive god, who accepted all traditions and blended them into one.

Now Passover and First Fruits, the festival of Yeshua's resurrection, would become The Feast of Ishtar, the goddess of fertility, or Easter with bunny rabbits and Easter eggs. (At that time eggs were dipped in the blood of the babies sacrificed to the goddess, thus the tradition of painting the eggs).

Now the fay of worship would change from Shabbat to Sunday in order to eternalize the sun god who for now would be called Jesus – yet it was another Jesus and certainly not Yeshua, the Jewish Messiah.

Then the day of the winter solstice of witchcraft, called Saturnalia or Paganalia, celebrated on the 25th of December in the Roman Empire, was to acquire the name Christmas and would celebrate the birth of this false Messiah. For the true Messiah was born during the holy biblical Feast of Tabernacles and followed the Hebrew biblical calendar, not the Roman one. (Daniel 7:25–27, Jeremiah 10:2–4 about the Christmas tree.)

The ancient Holy Book of the Hebrew Scriptures was to become obsolete, and its Laws done away with. Instead, Constantine compiled the apostolic writings, the letters of Paul and others into a new holy book and called it the New Testament. He gave this holy book his own perverse interpretation, completely divorced from the foundational Hebrew Writings whom he and his followers called the 'Old Testament.' (Matthew 5:17–21)

> "In rejecting their custom, we may transmit to our descendants the legitimate way of celebrating Easter... We ought not therefore to have anything in common with the Jew, for the Savior has shown us another way; our worship following a more legitimate and more convenient course (the order of the days of the week); And consequently, in unanimously adopting this mode, we desire dearest brethren to separate ourselves from the detestable company of the Jew." (Excerpt from *The Nicene Creed*, year 325, found in *Eusebius, Vita Const. Lib III 18-20*)

This creed and its instructions are still followed by most Christians today with the celebration of Easter, Christmas, Sunday (replacing Shabbat), and the rejection of the Laws of God.

Indeed, a new religion had been born. It had a gentile god by the name of Jesus Christ, an apostle by the name of Constantine, a new book by the name of the New Testament (although compiled from the apostolic writings, which are completely Yah-inspired, it was deceitfully interpreted through gentile eyes and gentile theologians), and new traditions, and unholy festivals such as Easter, Christmas, Sunday, and Halloween.

And most importantly... *no Jews*... no, not even the Messiah. What has been the fruit of this adulterous marriage?

**Either make the tree good and its fruit good, or else make the tree bad and its fruit bad; for a tree is known by its fruit.**

Matthew 12:33

The fruit of the first holy matrimony were salvations and healings. The fruit of this ungodly and pagan marriage were forced conversions and killings, yes even mass destructions of the family of Yeshua the Messiah, (the true Husband), in the name of the false Jesus Christ god created by Constantine.

A god who, according to Constantine in the Nicene Creed, had shown us *another way*. What was that way? It is a way of jealousy, hatred, killing, destruction, and Lawlessness. Horrendous Christian events such as pogroms, the holy inquisition, and the holocaust, have taken place since this ungodly 4th century marriage and the creation of this false religion.

The hatred conveyed in the Nicene Creed against the Jews and anything Jewish, including the Torah and the Old Testament, has continued through the great Protestant Reformation of the 16th century, and it still influences Christians today.

The following excerpt is from *Our Hands are Stained with Blood* by Michael Brown, as he quotes directly from Martin Luther's writings.

Luther wrote this after he was frustrated from trying to evangelize the Jews and when he was old and sick:

"What shall we Christians do with this damned rejected race of Jews? First, their synagogues should be set on fire. Secondly, their homes should likewise be broken down and destroyed. Thirdly, they should be deprived of their prayer books and Talmud's. Fourthly, their rabbis must be forbidden under threat of death to teach anymore. Fifthly, passports and traveling privileges should be absolutely forbidden to the Jews... To sum up dear princes and nobles, who have Jews in your domains, if this advice of mine does not suit you, then find a better one. So that you and we may all be free of this insufferable, devilish burden – the Jews." (Luther and Brown)

Hitler followed Luther's instructions meticulously and quoted him while doing so. The fruit? Over six million Jews exterminated in horrendous death camps and gas chambers, and many survivors scarred for life.

## Prophetic Altar Call

**After two days He will revive us; on the third day He will raise us up, that we may live in His sight. Let us know; let us pursue the knowledge of Yahveh. His going forth is established as the morning; He will come to us like the rain, like the latter and former rain to the earth.**

Hosea 6:2-3

The Third Day is upon us, the Third Millennium, and this is the Father's call to His Third Day church:
Come let us return to Yeshua, to our Jewish Messiah, His Jewish family and His ancient Hebrew Scriptures. Come let us

reinterpret the New Testament through the eyes of the holy Scriptures. Let us separate ourselves from our pagan husband, Constantine, and his false Jesus and let us go back to the true Messiah Yeshua, to His Father's Laws and Precepts, to true divine holy grace, to true love and holiness. Let us return to Jerusalem, and let us be made whole from centuries of adultery and paganism, as we go back to the original apostolic Jewish roots of our faith.

*In Yeshua's love and brokenness;*
**Archbishop Dr. Dominiquae & Rabbi Baruch Bierman**

Disclaimer: What this Article is Not Saying
- It is *not* saying to go back to the laws of Rabbinic Judaism.
- It is *not* implying that all Christians have anti-Semitism.
- It is *not* disqualifying the countless believers who call on the name of Jesus Christ meaning the *true* Jewish Messiah Yeshua.
- It is *not* disqualifying worship on Sunday, Monday, Tuesday or any other day.
- It is *not* disqualifying the New Testament as Bible (Only the wrong, 'divorced' interpretations of it).

# Bibliography

Brown, Michael L. *Our Hands Are Stained With Blood: The Tragic Story of the Church and the Jewish People.* Destiny Image Pub, 2019.

CFCA. "CFCA – 2017 Antisemitism Report – Present Situation and Tendencies." *CFCA,* 27 Jan. 2018, antisemitism.org.il/en/121652/. Accessed 6 July 2020.

CFI-USA. "In the Midst of All Shaking... – Christian Friends of Israel-USA." Cfi-Usa.Org, 2020, cfi-usa.org/in-the-midst-of-all-shaking/. Accessed 6 July 2020.

Excerpt from *The Nicene Creed*, year 325, found in *Eusebius, Vita Const. Lib III 18-20*

McTernan, John, Bill Koenig, and N. W. Hutchings. *Israel: The Blessing or the Curse.* Oklahoma City, OK: Hearthstone Publishing, 2002.

Rittner, Carol, Stephen D. Smith, Irena Steinfeldt, and Yehûdā Bauer. *The Holocaust and the Christian World: Reflections on the Past, Challenges for the Future.* New York: Paulist Press, 2019.

# Other Books by Archbishop Dr. Dominiquae Bierman

Order now online: www.kad-esh.org/shop/

*The MAP Revolution (Free E-Book)*
Find Out Why Revival Does Not Come... Yet!

*The Identity Theft*
The Return of the 1st Century Messiah

*The Healing Power of the Roots*
It's a Matter of Life or Death!

*Grafted In*
The Return to Greatness

*Restoring the Glory: The Original Way*
The Ancient Paths Rediscovered

*Stormy Weather*
Judgment Has Already Begun, Revival is Knocking at the Door

*Yeshua is the Name*
The Important Restoration of the Original Hebrew Name of the Messiah

*The Bible Cure for Africa and the Nations*
The Key to the Restoration of All Africa

*The Key of Abraham*
The Blessing or the Curse?

*Yes!*
The Dramatic Salvation of Archbishop Dr. Dominiquae Bierman

*Eradicating the Cancer of Religion*
Hint: All People Have It

*Restoration of Holy Giving*
Releasing the True 1,000 Fold Blessing

*Vision Negev*
The Awesome Restoration of the Sephardic Jews

*Defeating Depression*
This Book is a Kiss from Heaven

*From Sickology to a Healthy Logic*
The Product of 18 Years Walking Through Psychiatric Hospitals

*ATG: Addicts Turning to God*
The Biblical Way to Handle Addicts and Addictions

*The Woman Factor by Rabbi Baruch Bierman*
Freedom From Womanphobia

*The Revival of the Third Day (Free E-Book)*
The Return to Yeshua the Jewish Messiah

## Music Albums
www.kad-esh.org/shop/

*The Key of Abraham*

*Abba Shebashamayim*

*Uru*

*Retorno*

# Get Equipped & Partner with Us

### Global Revival MAP (GRM) Israeli Bible School
Take the most comprehensive video Bible school online that focuses on dismantling replacement theology.
For more information or to order, please contact us:
www.grmbibleschool.com | grm@dominiquaebierman.com

### United Nations for Israel Movement
We invite you to join us as a member and partner with $25 a month, which supports the advancing of this End time vision that will bring true unity to the body of the Messiah. We will see the One New Man form, witness the restoration of Israel, and take part in the birthing of Sheep Nations.
Today is an exciting time to be serving Him!
www.unitednationsforisrael.org | info@unitednationsforisrael.org

### Global Re-Education Initiative (GRI) Against Anti-Semitism
Discover the Jewishness of Jesus and defeat Christian anti-Semitism with this online video course to see revival in your nation!
www.against-antisemitism.com | info@against-antisemitism.com

*Join Our Annual Israel Tours*
Travel through the Holy Land and watch
the Hebrew Holy Scriptures come alive.
www.kad-esh.org/tours-and-events/

*To Send Offerings to Support our Work*
Your help keeps this mission of restoration *going far and wide!*
www.kad-esh.org/donations

**CONTACT US**
Archbishop Dr. Dominiquae & Rabbi Baruch Bierman
Kad-Esh MAP Ministries | www.kad-esh.org
info@kad-esh.org

United Nations for Israel | www.unitednationsforisrael.org
info@unitednationsforisrael.org

Zions Gospel Press | shalom@zionsgospel.com
52 Tuscan Way, Ste 202-412, 32092
St. Augustine Florida, USA | +1-972-301-7087

www.ingramcontent.com/pod-product-compliance
Lightning Source LLC
Chambersburg PA
CBHW021426070526
44577CB00001B/80